SCOTCH MISSED

SCOTCH MISSED

The Lost Distilleries of Scotland

BRIAN TOWNSEND

NEIL WILSON PUBLISHING

Published by Neil Wilson Publishing Ltd
303a, The Pentagon Centre
36 Washington Street
GLASGOW G3 8AZ
Tel: 0141-221-1117
Fax: 0141-221-5363
E-mail: nwp@cqm.co.uk
http://www.nwp.co.uk/

A catalogue record for this book is available from the British Library.

ISBN 1-897784-53-8

Designed by Janet Watson

Printed in Malta by Interprint

All photographs have been credited where possible but many are of unknown provenance. The remainder have been taken by the author.

Contents

To those who once worked
in Scotland's lost distilleries

PREFACE

It is over 500 years since distilling took root in Scotland and more than 200 years since it became an organised industry. As such it has known two golden ages of growth, the late 19th century and the years from 1950–80, and few doubt that the next age of growth is more than a decade away.

However like all industries, distilling has known its bad times, in particular the years from 1909–33 when everything to do with whisky went sour. Strong spirits were seen as the root of all social evil and a global wave against 'likker' brought distilling in Scotland and elsewhere to its knees.

Taxation purposely priced whisky out of people's pockets and the United States, Scotch's number one export market, prohibited the sale of alcohol from January 1920. In a speech to the Federation of British Industry (forerunner of the CBI) in 1921, the chairman of the giant Distillers Company Ltd (DCL), William Ross, horrified his audience by saying the situation was so grave that 50 to 100 distilleries would have to close in the next decade.

He was to be proved right. From 170 distilleries in the toping 1880s, the tally fell to around 40 in 1933. For a few brief black months the number of functioning distilleries actually dropped to single figures.

In a way, Ireland's tragedy was greater. In the early 1920s, it lost its US market through prohibition, its home market through leaving the United Kingdom, so 28 distilleries were to shrink to just two, just one of them in the republic. Only now, 70 years on, is Irish distilling finally making some headway again.

Not all distilleries listed in this book closed during the maelstrom of the 1920s, but most of them did. Those which closed at other times had their own sad stories to tell, too. Some had problems of water supply, others were too isolated, some were badly run, some produced whisky that did not please the changing public palate. Some had a run of old-fashioned bad luck. In all, almost 100 of them have closed, each one taking with it a dram of lost Scottish history. This book tries to record some of that history and bring it back to life.

The Scots have always been a race with a deep sense of family and kinship. In few domains is this sense of family as pronounced as in whisky-making. The history of the industry is also one of the great whisky families such as Stein, Haig, Usher, Grant, Walker, Calder, McDonald, Greenlees, Colville and many, many others whose names crop up again and again in the archives of so many distilleries.

However, it has not been possible to include every family link and connection with each lost distillery. To have done so would have meant creating a book of encyclopaedic length. Each lost distillery has its own pen portrait, but a full Bayeux Tapestry of their role in the industry's development must wait for another day and another book.

I would like to acknowledge the help and support of the following people without whom this book would never have completed. They are: James Stephens, Auchtertool, Fife; Moffat Reid, Falkirk; Murdo Macdonald, archivist, Lochgilphead; Charles Sharpe, until recently manager of Lochside Distillery, Montrose, and finally Neil Wilson for backing the idea and Alan Winchester, now at Aberlour Distillery, for his tireless delving and unfathomable memory.

Brian Townsend
Kirkinch, Meigle
March 1997

Introduction

The Scotch whisky industry is one of the wonders of the world and the product it makes is one of the world's most enduring success stories. True, whisky is made in many countries but it is wholly and indissolubly linked to one country, Scotland.

There are other drinks and spirits which have a similar apparent link with one country. We talk, for instance, of Jamaica rum, French wine and Russian vodka. But these do not have the remarkable, almost reflex linkage that the two words 'Scotch' and 'whisky' have in the minds of a large slice of humankind. To many people all over the world, there is only one true whisky and that is Scotch.

Whiskies are now produced in dozens, indeed scores, of other countries, from the United States to Spain, from Canada to Korea, from Japan to Brazil. But Scotch somehow seems to stand and remain head and shoulders above the others. It is a product that has acquired a timeless mystique that has transformed this once-crude distillate of fermented barley into one of the marvels of the world. It is simply the world's most successful spirit and most universally-known strong alcoholic drink.

Repair to a watering hole anywhere from Buffalo to Bulawayo, from Darwin to Davos, from the Arctic Circle to Tierra del Fuego and it will sell at least one brand of Scotch, usually three or four, sometimes a dozen. People drink it by itself, with water or ice, with soda or ginger ale, Coke or other mixers. It has invaded films, television and the tough, hard-boiled American novel as well as the war novel, the spy thriller, the whodunnit and the potboiler to name but a few.

There may be exotic cocktails drunk by some Caribbean pool-side, superb chateau-bottled clarets served with hautest of haute cuisine aboard the Orient Express, the finest of cognacs served in snifters big enough to float a toy yacht in, but those appear once – just before the hero carries the damsel off to a night of passion between the sheets. For the rest of the novel, Scotch rules the roost. Among characters as disparate as Raymond Chandler's Philip Marlowe and John le Carré's Alec Leamas, Scotch is the oiler of human cogwheels, the yardstick currency of hospitality, the soma that knits up the ravelled sleeve of care. There is hardly a 20th-century novel or film which does not contain one scene of two people warily getting to know each other when one character stalks across to the drinks tray or cabinet and says: 'What'll you have? Scotch?'

What is fascinating is how the seeds of this universal success story were sown in an age when marketing and advertising were in their infancy. Furthermore this conquest of drinkers' palates has been achieved by a drink that in essence is simply made of water, barley and yeast. Yet somehow this unlikely drink has made itself into a kind of bottled global ambassador. If one were asked to create the proverbial time capsule of the late 20th century containing a dozen or more items embodying life as we know it today, a bottle of Scotch would doubtless be on the list, possibly with a video cassette, a compact disc and a Honda motorcycle. Were the time capsule unearthed two centuries hence, those other items might be relatively unknown to the archaeologists of the year 2200; but I would bet a hogshead of single malt to a bottle of supermarket blend they would have no trouble identifying the bottle of whisky.

However, what we tend to forget about Scotland's great liquid asset is that, for all its taste, fascination and mystique, Scotch and its manufacture is an industry – and one which has known bad times as well as good. Indeed, some of its bad times have seen it pushed to the verge of extinction. We tend to forget when we buy a bottle at the supermarket or the off-licence that behind that flagon lies a vast commercial supply line of maltings and distilleries, bonded stores, bottling and packaging plants and a worldwide network of distributors. In the bad times, many of the places linked to the making of whisky were closed down, either short-term or for good.

Of these, the distilleries represent a special loss. Many had their own characteristics which in turn meant they produced a uniquely-flavoured malt whisky. Each one had its own combination of location, malting, stills used, water sources, peat and barley. Finally, the most important ingredient was the character of the men who made the Scotch, whose skills, experience, faults and idiosyncrasies all added to the flavour of the final product.

As a result of the bad times over the past century, about 100 distilleries have closed in Scotland. Of these, two dozen or so have reopened, some after having stood idle for nigh on two generations.

But more than 70 have not reopened – and it is about them this book is written. The reasons for their permanent closure are many and varied – though the vast majority closed during the supremely difficult 20 years from the start of World War I through to the Great Depression of 1929-34.

With the benefit of hindsight it must be said that the terrible cull of distilleries which peaked in the 1920s and early 1930s – largely organised and orchestrated by the Distillers Company Ltd (better known as DCL) under their gaunt, austere director William Ross – probably saved the industry. Had it not been done, the global success of Scotch whisky today might not have taken place.

However, these lost distilleries represent an important part of Scotland's industrial history and national heritage. Many have been partly demolished or have been changed to other uses. Some have been razed and every vestige of their existence obliterated. All are interesting in their own way. Some have fascinating histories behind them. Some were the settings for great human dramas. Some were landmarks in the industry's own history. A few are still almost complete with all the equipment still there, as if in a deep trance waiting for the day when an owner might decide the time was right to restoke the fires and breathe warm life again into the cold stills.

I could not see that happening when I wrote the original edition of *Scotch Missed* in 1993 and indeed I feared the opposite. The global recession of the early 1990s had curtailed the demand for Scotch, and there was said to be overcapacity and overstocking, though not as severe as in the early 1980s. Older, less efficient malt distilleries still continue to be under scrutiny at a time when the company accountant and the bottom line rule supreme. A distillery that sires a great-name single malt is likely to be safe enough – Ardbeg's recent sale to Glenmorangie plc is an example of this – a distillery that produces a reasonable but unnoted malt for the blenders may well be at risk, especially if it is an old and inefficient plant.

The other problem is that a malt distillery is a very long-term investment. Output compared to a big grain distillery is modest and it will be many years before today's output can legally be sold as whisky. Faced with the accountant's preference for short-term returns rather than long-term growth, a private individual or small consortium gaining the necessary backing to rekindle the fires of a mothballed distillery is unlikely. But I note that there were interested parties in the Ardbeg sale who were not big distilling organisations.

So maybe the tide is turning a little and the booming worldwide interest in high quality bottled malt will result in some of our mothballed plants being brought back to life. Certainly, my initial pessimism has been checked a little by these revelations and I am now more hopeful about the future.

Having said that, I still expect more additions to the list of lost distilleries in this book, although the present situation pales into insignificance compared to the woes that beset the Scotch whisky industry in the first third of the 20th century. However, before we portray these lost distilleries in detail, we need to trace the industry from its rural and illegal roots to its high water mark in the last decade of Queen Victoria's reign.

It is not within this book's scope to describe that history in detail – but I will try to provide a usable framework. I have also concluded that readers of *Scotch Missed* would rather drink their whisky than read a chemistry lesson on how it is made; there are enough books on the market which describe this process adequately. However, I will touch upon some of the production processes in chapter one, in particular with reference to how our Victorian predecessors might have carried them out.

So pour a good dram, perhaps from one of the distilleries in this book, and let's go in search of *Scotch Missed.*

TURNING BACK THE CLOCK

I do not wish to dwell on the processes involved when whisky is made but it is worth noting briefly how it was done 100 years ago, if only to appreciate the long, arduous and labour-intensive task it then was. Today, a vast modern fully-automated distillery can produce millions of gallons a year with just a handful of staff. In bygone times, a distillery had to employ as many as 20 people for an annual output of 100,000 gallons or less.

One contemporary description of whisky-making appeared in the *Lothian Courier* in August, 1877, written by a journalist who had visited Glenmavis near Bathgate. Glenmavis was a farm-based Lowland malt distillery, as were many at the time, built on a long sloping site beside a water source. However, uniquely among malt distilleries it had installed a Coffey patent still in 1855. That apart, the following description could have applied to the vast majority of malt distilleries in the later Victorian era. In addition, it is typical of the fawning style awash with flowery circumlocutions beloved of writers of the period.

> *We were kindly privileged to go through the distillery and were shown the different gradations through which the grain has to pass before it is made into good malt whisky. It is proper to state at the outset that nothing but barley is used at Glenmavis in making the malt and the process, as far as we are able to detail it, may not be uninteresting.*
>
> *The barley is first put into the steep for the purpose of being softened, where it remains for about seventy-two hours. It is then casted in the couch, where it remains for twenty-four hours. It is afterwards spread out upon the young floor, where it remains for*

some time, and thence removed to the old floor for the purpose of germination.

After about nine days it is shifted to the kiln where it remains for forty-eight hours. After being dried on the kiln, it is shifted into a place called the malt deposit or store-room. From the malt deposit the malt, as it is now called, is removed to the malt store. Thence it is lowered to the mill room where it is ground with a first-class engine.

The malt is next put in to the mash tun and hot water let in upon it from the copper. It is stirred by a machine and the draff let off. The liquid wort being run into coolers, it is allowed to cool down to a certain degree of heat before it goes into the wash backs for fermentation.

After being properly fermented, it is removed to a place called the wash charger, thence it is removed to the still. The still is one of Coffey's patent apparatus. After the wash is distilled, it becomes spirits, which are removed to the spirit receiver, whence the spirits are filled into casks for consumption and deposited in the warehouse or bond, to be kept there till required. About six weeks are required to complete the process.

Mr MacNab (the proprietor) makes his whisky from pure malt only. The machinery connected with the works is wrought both by steam and water power at intervals. The warehouses are of a very extensive nature and the barrels have a very formidable appearance as to size and number. There could not be fewer than a thousand of them, all filled with the best Glenmavis Malt Whisky.

It may surprise the readers of this journal when they are told that every quarter of barley Mr MacNab uses yields to the Inland Revenue Department of the Government £9 of duty, or in other words that the gentleman adds fifty thousand pounds a year to the revenue, taking it all in all. This is no exaggeration, but plain facts and figures. It may be mentioned that Glenmavis distillery has been in the possession of Mr MacNab and his late worthy father for nearly half a century.

Had Glenmavis kept its original pot stills, the distillation process would have involved a large wash still and a smaller spirit still. In fact, many lowland malts were, and still are, triple-distilled. What prompted the MacNabs to install a Coffey still is a moot point.

Certainly in terms of size and output, Glenmavis was too small to make effective use of it, as Coffey stills were most effective at bulk grain distilling.

Malt whisky distilling today is fundamentally not that different, although most aspects of the process are more efficient. Relatively few distilleries today make their own malt – the process is done on an industrial scale in vast maltings, such as can be found at Kirkcaldy, Port Ellen and Portgordon, to name but three. Milling the malt is still done at the distillery, with the grist and hot water being mixed in vast mash tuns or Lauter tuns with mechanical stirrers helping to agitate and thus extract every last gram of maltose from the hot liquor which is known as wort.

This is then collected in the underbacks, pumped via coolers into the washbacks where yeast is added and the fermentation process begins at a controlled temperature with mechanical whisks or switchers skimming the resultant froth. The fully-fermented wort is known as the wash which is then pumped via the wash charger into the wash still, which usually contains revolving rummagers to prevent the wash sticking and scorching on the still walls. The still may be heated directly by coal or gas but more frequently this is done indirectly by an internal coil of steam-heated pipes. The spirit vapour rises up the neck of the still into the lyne arm where it begins to condense and then runs off through a condenser (most frequently the worm tub in Victorian distilleries) and into the low wines and feints charger. This weak spirit is then passed into the spirit still and redistilled. The first portion of condensed vapour from this still is held back as the foreshots for redistillation and when the desired alcoholic volume in the condensate is reached – the middle cut – this is diverted into the spirit receiver via the spirit safe. When the strength begins to drop, the condensate is diverted back into the low wines and feints charger for reprocessing. The spirit in the receiver is then casked and put into bond. At some modern distilleries there are no bonded warehouses on site, so the spirit is loaded into road tankers and taken to central bonds some distance away.

Several additional considerations affect distilling today – the need to preserve energy, increase output, avoid environmental pollution and to find a market – or at least a commercial use – for all waste products. Whisky-making is highly energy-intensive, with heat being used to malt the barley, work the stills and produce the hot water for mashing. A generation ago, it was reckoned it took a gallon of fuel oil to make a gallon of whisky. Today the figure is down to well under half a gallon and falling thanks to better heating systems, good insulation and innovative use of heat exchangers. Bowmore in Islay uses much of its waste heat to fuel the kiln and also heat the local swimming pool!

Increased production is achieved by more automation of the distillation processes, more stills – though not necessarily larger ones – and constant detailed improvements to every aspect of production. Industry research has also looked at making the mash, worts and wash more concentrated to increase the alcohol-water ratio and thus cut energy needed for distillation. However, some short cuts have been found to alter the spirit flavour and are thus either abandoned or modified.

Distilleries are great consumers of water and, in an age where the 'true environmental cost' of any industry is under scrutiny, distillers are having to look both at the water they require and the used waters they release as waste. For years, certain distilleries dumped pot ale and spent lees (the watery residue from the second distillation in the spirit still) into adjacent rivers or the sewage system with little regard for the consequences. But with both UK and EU standards getting ever tighter, those days are long since at an end.

The other main by-product, draff, has always sold readily to livestock farmers. Whisky makers have long known that pot ale, for all its glutinous appearance and pungent smell, is rich in nutrients. The idea of mixing draff and pot ale, then heating and compressing the mix into cake pellets or 'dark grains' as cattle feed dates back many years and is finally coming into its own. Today most distilleries have their own dark grains plant or jointly operate one with neighbouring or linked distilleries.

Certain things remain unchanged, however. Whisky is still stored in wooden barrels for a minimum of three years in bond (that is, duty unpaid) until it departs to the blenders, for bulk export overseas or is bottled as single malt. Blending remains as skilled and mysterious a craft as ever and blended whiskies, despite the steep rise to prominence of single malts in recent years, still dominate the markets by a ratio of 10:1 in the UK, even higher elsewhere. One big growth area in recent years is in supermarkets' own-label whisky, with some chains now offering standard, aged and de luxe blends, plus their own unnamed Speyside, Islay, Lowland and Campbeltown single malts. Tesco even offers a house single grain whisky. Vatted malts, which are blended solely from a handful of malts, are also on the increase, as are de luxe blends with a higher than normal percentage of malt.

The success of Scotch whisky still defies accurate analysis. It is also an industry awash with paradox. It is among the world's most sophisticated industries, yet it is also steeped in tradition. It is taxed oppressively, yet in real terms it is as cheap as at any time this century. It is an industry that thinks in millions of gallons, yet the customer resolutely buys one bottle at a time. It is an industry capitalised in billions of pounds on the stock market yet a few pence on the pub dram can send sales into a nosedive.

Finally, it is an industry with an enduring mystery. There are scores of malt distilleries all carrying out the same process with the same barley and yeast in tanks and stills made by the same manufacturers. Yet no single malt ever tastes exactly like another – and distilleries only yards apart using the same water and peat can produce utterly dissimilar whiskies.

Like all industries, Scotch whisky owes its success to moving with the times, developing new ideas, finding new markets, expanding to meet demand but contracting in adversity. Such periods of adversity were mainly responsible for most of Scotland's lost distilleries, although each distillery closure had its own special human and historical side to it. It is the human side, scant records and failing memories of old men permitting, I have tried to chronicle.

Out of the Farmyards. . .

The earliest whisky distilled in this part of the world was almost certainly made in Ireland. The technique came to Scotland, most probably via Islay in the late 15th century. For generations it was very much a small scale industry based around the croft and farmyard with almost wholly local markets being serviced. Distilling was considered a birthright and in the 16th and 17th centuries the island chieftains could produce large quantities of 'home-brew' for their own household's consumption without fear of breaking any law. Not that they would have cared anyway since the island clans were very much a law unto themselves. This attitude to officialdom coupled with distilling, traditionally percolated down through generations until it manifested itself most visibly in the sometimes comic capers between the smugglers, illicit distillers and excisemen in the 18th and 19th centuries. These parties fought a battle of guile and attrition that in retrospect seems an absurd waste of human endeavour. But there was a great deal at stake. The Scots Parliament first levied a duty on ale in 1644 at a rate of two shillings and eight pence per Scots pint. Ostensibly, this was to finance the expenses of the Royalist army. After that, every successive government has recognised the revenue-raising value of alcohol in all its forms.

Alcohol was thus the guinea pig for the first bulk system of indirect taxation. But people in bygone times were even more reluctant to pay their taxes than we are today – and making them pay was more difficult. It became a national sport to evade taxes by all and every means, especially those taxes levied on alcohol.

After the Act of Union of 1707 the Excise Board was created with strong powers to raise revenue, particularly on alcohol and tobacco, throughout the new United Kingdom of England, Wales, Scotland and Ireland. But perhaps through an administrative oversight, the island of Islay was omitted from the Excise Board's powers. Collection of revenues there was 'farmed' out to the laird, Daniel Campbell of Shawfield, who strongly encouraged distilling as a sure and certain source of revenue, just as his successors were to do for many years. For that and its geographical features – an abundance of peat moss and soft, peat-darkened rivers – Islay became and still is the isle of whisky par excellence.

For nearly 120 years after 1707, Parliament and successive governments blundered around trying to find a formula that would allow the growing distilling industry to work efficiently, that would maximise revenue and discourage illicit distilling and smuggling. One cannot say they were successful. Duties on spirits rose and fell like Solway tides. They frequently varied depending on whether the spirits were distilled in England, Ireland and Scotland. Scotland was split by the notorious 'Highland Line' which ran roughly between Greenock and Dundee, with different terms and conditions applying to distillers on either side of it. There was rarely, if ever, a free market. Some Scots distillers had permission to sell to English buyers, others had not. Highland distillers – those north of the line – were not allowed to sell to the Lowlands of Scotland. To aggravate matters, the rules often changed from year to year. There were strict laws on the size of stills – laws which changed with monotonous regularity and high, sometimes formidable, annual levies based on their capacity. This led to shallow, low-capacity stills and high-speed distilling and recharging (as much as four times an hour). The result was usually vile-tasting whisky and scorched, ill-cleaned stills. On top of all that, Scotland during the 1790s and first decades of the 19th century was afflicted by several years of foul weather and abysmal harvests. These caused widespread famine, with barley (or the northern variety, called 'bere' or 'bigg') in very short supply. In some years, Parliament had to outlaw the use of barley for brewing and distilling; every grain harvested was needed for human consumption. Throughout that era, illicit distilling was rampant, particularly in the Highlands, Islands and rebellious Ireland.

Few tales of social history can match the relentless battle of wits which was fought in Scotland and Ireland between the excisemen or 'gaugers', and the distillers and smugglers. To evade the gaugers' all-pervading eyes, stills were installed in ever-more remote bothies, caves and forsaken glens. Whisky barrels were lashed to the backs of horses or ponies and carried in the dead of night to towns and villages, with sacks of barley or malt carried back to ensure the production of the next batch.

The ingenuity of the illicit distillers knew no bounds – one distiller ran a smoke-flue half a mile underground from his still in a secret cave to his cottage chimney where it would not attract the gaugers' attention. Such was the demand for illicit spirit that many people, even men of the cloth, became involved. Tales abound, too many to relate here, but one of the better known illustrates the genre well and involved the Rev. Magnus Eunson who ran a still in Orkney, the notoriety of which reached the ears of the excisemen who resolved to raid it. However, thanks to the island's bush telegraph that operated then as now, the minister got wind of the impending swoop. With scant time to spare, three barrels of whisky were stood upright, covered with a white cloth and a coffin placed on top. A dozen parishioners were rushed in to act as bereaved and mourners. The excisemen arrived in mid-funeral service – and a whisper from one 'mourner' that the deceased had died of smallpox was enough to send the gaugers hastily away.

Equal ingenuity was applied to smuggling. Both excisemen and smugglers – who were usually distillers as well – went to great lengths to outwit each other. It even reached the pitch that smugglers would send out decoy parties of two barrel-laden horses and men in advance to attract the attention of the gaugers. Once spotted, the men would run for it, heading into the wilds to put up a great fight, only eventually to be overpowered. The excisemen would return in triumph with their captures, not realising that a score or 40 horses had safely got through while they were otherwise engaged.

Life was tough for both sides. Crofters were driven to illicit distilling by the harshness and poverty of their lives; it was one effective way of 'adding value' to the meagre output of their crofts. Their dire circumstances were often seen and understood by the Justices of the Peace who sentenced them in court. The JPs were usually landowners – and many were among the illegal distillers' most regular customers. Sentences imposed were often lenient and minimal, the charges often dismissed. However, it did not mean an illicit distiller got off scot-free. Usually the excisemen confiscated or destroyed his still, so he had to find the money to buy another.

Life for the excisemen was equally tough. They might have to spend weeks trying to pin down and arrest an illicit distiller or smuggler. Often that meant employing armed men – and paying them out of their own pockets. An exciseman's pay was linked to the number of successful prosecutions he made and the amount levied by the courts in fines. As the fines imposed were often derisory, excisemen found it a hard and precarious living. Many became quite demoralised. With the benefit of hindsight it might also be argued that, in an age of hardship and difficulty, the whole thing was a great waste of human resources.

This unabated mutual conflict continued until the 1820s, when two great Acts were passed that changed the face of distilling in Britain. These were the Excise Act of 1823 and the Repeal of the Corn Laws 25 years later. The latter effectively scrapped taxes on cereal crops and freed the importing of barley and other grain from foreign countries – particularly from North America. The former Act made it truly viable for the first time to distil legally in the United Kingdom. The combination of the two lured countless people to register as distillers, including many former illicit distillers and smugglers. However, illicit distilling continued in the Highlands, though at a reduced level, for much of the last century. During the 1820s, distilling became the gold-rush industry. Hundreds of companies were set up, almost all of which eventually went bust. Among the survivors was one Johnny Walker, born in 1820, but his company was an exception. Hundreds of others went, appositely, down the drain.

Not all failed companies were badly run or produced poor whisky – though that applied in many cases. There were simply too many distillers producing too much product for the market, even in a state of flux, to absorb. There was a parallel in the 1980s, when hundreds of people stampeded into software or video retailing. For every firm that succeeded, dozens failed.

Most new distilleries were small, two-stilled affairs resembling farmyard outbuildings – indeed many of them were exactly that. Some were marginally larger and a handful were industrially-scaled distilleries with considerable financial backing to them. In addition, there were several big distilleries which had been operating in the Lowlands since the mid-1700s, mainly owned by the powerful Haig and Stein dynasties, who were the earliest successful bulk distillers. Many were to fail only to be rebuilt on a grander scale with influxes of new capital. Many successful distilleries like Laphroaig in Islay underwent rebuilding in the mid to late Victorian era which ensured that although their beginnings were modest, their futures were as assured as their owners could make them. That many of them still survive is a tribute to their owners' foresight during that time. Of the distilleries that did fail in the post-1823 shake-out, most were small, isolated and under-capitalised. But in their brief lives and early demise they spelled out to others the risks and hazards of the new unfettered industry. The lessons did not go unlearned and many of the distilleries which survived were to thrive until the end of the 19th century and beyond.

Growth Into The Golden Era

Historians can look at the growth of a nation, industry or company and see it as a clear, logical, inevitable path through the landscape of time. But when crucial events happened, there was nothing clear, logical or inevitable about them to the people closely involved. Such is the case of Scotland in the 19th century, when whisky had its first true golden age. However, there was also a great element of historical fortuity and luck.

To potential whisky distillers, the 1823 Excise Act set out three things. To be legal, the minimum still size was 40 gallons. The legislators hope was that stills of such volume would remain in situ and could not be removed and reinstated as quickly as the illicit stills were. A distilling licence cost £10 a year and there was a half-crown excise duty per gallon, well down from the five shillings and sixpence duty before the Act. If whisky was exported – and that included to England – there was a rebate of threepence a gallon. For the first time in British history, said a generally approving press, it was viable to distil legally.

The 1823 Act also coincided, give or take a few years, with the industrial revolution and the coming of the railways. The former saw great strides forward in metallurgy which meant far larger copper stills could be manufactured at reasonable cost. Great boilers could now provide ample hot water to extract the sugars from the malt and steam to heat the stills. The repeal of the Corn Laws meant barley could be bought at realistic prices in a wider market. The railways and steam-powered coastal shipping ensured large quantities of barley and coal could be transported to the distilleries – even the quite remote ones in the Hebrides – and barrels and hogsheads of their golden nectar shipped to distant buyers and consumers.

Of course, all this did not happen overnight. Right up until the end of the 19th century, many Scots and Irish distilleries still sold their output by the barrel to local pubs, inns and licensed victuallers and hardly sold further afield. A grocer or merchant in a village or town might stock four or five barrels of different local malts, identified by a card tacked to each one.

A typical card might read *MacFadyen's Glen Zoar finest Highland malt, two years old, 95 proof, 2/- a pint, 3/11d a quart.* Customers came in with jugs, pitchers or flasks and these were filled directly from the barrel, measured in handsome if battered copper measuring jugs kept by the merchant. A similar system, using a wider range of measures, prevailed at the public house.

Old-fashioned as it seems, it is a system that has survived into living memory in other European countries. I remember choosing and buying brandy from the barrel at bodegas in Spain in the mid-1960s – and there are Mediterranean countries where grocers to this day sell local wines from barrels direct from the vineyard.

This system of supplying to local outlets was typical of many farmyard distilleries. Some of the most romantic and delightful lost distilleries belong in this category. Others also operated as breweries: after all, the initial stages of making beer and whisky are very similar, as are those of wine and brandy making. Devanha in Aberdeen and Glenaden at Old Deer, Aberdeenshire, were two locations where a brewery and distillery worked in tandem. Lochside in Montrose, due to be demolished as a distillery, was once also a brewery.

Indeed, in the liveliest period of 19th century growth, early maltings were built using ideas and techniques linked to brewing. Old photographs show more than one 19th-century Scottish malt kiln with conical towers surmounted by donkey's-ear vents copied straight from Kentish oasthouses. However, in 1889 Charles Chree Doig, an architect who worked out of Elgin, was asked by the owners of Dailuaine Distillery to design a new maltings plant to cope with increasing demand. His first attempt was a slatted box-like structure but he drew a line through this and developed it into a pagoda roof which prominently topped the 80-foot high kiln until 1917 when it was destroyed by fire, a year before Doig died. The innovation of Doig's design was immediately recognised by the *Wine Trade Review* and Doig incorporated the pagoda top into all of his subsequent designs.

Going into distilling was a logical step for farmers. Many had good water sources on site, a peat moss nearby and under-utilised byres and other farm buildings. There was usually a ready market for whisky on their doorstep. Distilling offered a far better return on investment than selling grain to mills or other outlets. True, it was not as simple as that and virtually all genuine farm distilleries have disappeared. But Annandale, Jericho/Benachie, Glenaden, Auchnagie, Ballechin and Glenmavis knew success in their time.

While the industrial revolution and improved transport played their part in the industry's growth, a handful of inventions and fortuitous events also contributed to the tale. Four in particular stand out. They are the invention of Coffey's patent still; the great blight, phylloxera, which devastated France's vineyards; the mass production of cheap glass bottles; and the concept of blending.

Experts and whisky historians could spend hours, doubtless with brimming glass to hand, debating which of these four was most crucial to the industry's success. My own view, based purely on affection for one of history's most underrated inventors, is that Aeneas Coffey and his still deserve the accolade. A friend of mine once said of him: 'For someone who did so much for the Scotch whisky industry, he had three things going against him: he was Irish, he was an exciseman and his name was Coffey.'

However, Ireland had several centuries' head start in distilling over Scotland – and as recently as 1900, there were still almost 30 distilleries operating there. Mr Coffey was head of the British Customs and Excise in Dublin in the 1820s and – like many other people connected with distilling – was very aware of how inefficient the universal pot still process was at that time.

As I outlined in chapter one, a pot still had to be filled with fermented wash, the fire or boiler had to be stoked up, the spirit vapour condensed and then only the middle cut of any distillation was generally used for further distillation or casking. The fire or boiler then had to be damped down, the still cooled and recharged and the process repeated. Every so often the process had to be stopped so the pot ale could be cleaned out. Incidentally, this was a very hazardous process, as pot ale gave off toxic fumes which displaced the air in the still. Many distillery workers died during this operation.

Then the whole process, charging, firing up and distilling started all over again. It meant a still only did its main task for a few hours a day. Speeding matters up by using shallow stills increased output, but the resultant spirit often tasted utterly vile. Added to all that, a percentage of the spirit tended to get lost or wasted in the process.

The Stein system developed in the 1820s – which had three linked pot-stills working simultaneously – overcame some shortcomings, but was seen by many as a complicated palliative.

Patented in 1830, Coffey's patent still was a bigger, far more complex device – but a far more efficient one. It is a tribute to its design that patent stills made today, though better in many details, are largely the same as Coffey's original concept. Analogies between different industries are difficult, but one could say Aeneas Coffey was the Henry Ford of distilling.

The patent still had two sections, usually separate high columns called the analyser and the rectifier. Hot alcoholic wash cascaded from the top of the analyser over layers of perforated plates while steam was allowed in at the bottom. Strong alcohol vapour and steam came off at the top while a spirit-free residue flowed away below. The hot vapour was ducted across to the rectifier where it was cooled by pipes containing cold, incoming wash which, as with the pot still, ensured that the alcohol – of high purity – condensed and flowed out as a clear stream.

Coffey's still outshone the pot still on three counts. It was more efficient, it produced purer alcohol and it could run for days on end without the need for maintenance and regular cleaning.

Its disadvantages included high initial cost, the resultant whisky lacked character and flavour and the fact that it worked best only in long production runs. This made it very difficult to operate in small rural distilleries. The result was that large urban distilleries, which could produce the volumes of wash needed for the Coffey stills, were the first to adopt them. In turn, it often proved difficult to obtain the necessary quantities of malted barley to feed these big stills.

The breakthrough came from the US in the shape of corn on the cob or maize, which the Americans had started using as a cheap raw material for their distilleries. They found that maize, steam-cooked until the kernels and starch cells burst, then mixed with malting barley in a 4:1 ratio, produced a strong wash suitable for distillation in Coffey stills and Irish pot stills.

This product, based on 80% maize and 20% barley, became the staple output of the big urban distilleries. Named grain whisky, it began to overshadow malt whisky. It was far cheaper, often smoother and tended to be a more consistent product in an era when the quality of many malt whiskies varied widely from year to year or even from distillation to distillation.

On the other hand, grain whisky – from vast, anonymous distilleries in central Glasgow and Edinburgh, or even Liverpool and Manchester – tended to be anodyne and lacked the flavour, character and charisma of the Highland and Island malts.

However, unlike the malt distillers, grain distillers were not stuck with producing whisky alone. By re-distilling grain whisky they could produce cheap rectified spirit that was the ideal base for gin, a British copy of the Dutch juniper-flavoured spirit, genever. Genever had been an imported popular spirit for nearly a century and gin had long been on the market as a low-cost home-produced substitute. Heady, potent and cheap – at a penny a gill in the scruffy taverns of London's East End and elsewhere – it became a very widespread drink, especially among working-class women. Not entirely in jest did gin get the nickname 'Mother's Ruin'.

By the mid-19th century, the UK spirits market was a strange, stratified place. As a rough rule of thumb, the upper classes drank brandy and the poor drank gin. There was a good market for rum, especially in towns with a naval tradition. The whisky market was split between big urban distillers offering bland but reliable grain whisky and the fragmented malt distillers who sold their output to local customers or, thanks to the growth of whisky merchants, to discerning clients in the far away cities. Like ale, whisky was supplied to retail outlets in barrels which were bulky, awkward and took up a lot of space. Things were improved by the invention of the whisky-jar. This was a samovar-like glass urn with a capacity of about one or two gallons and a tap at the bottom. It was filled from the barrel and sat on the pub bar or behind it. But the whisky it contained was not 'brand whisky' as we know it today – it was simply whatever the landlord had in his barrels in the store-room or cellar.

Whisky was doing all right, but was very much an also-ran in a race with no clear favourite. By the 1890s, however, whisky's standing would be transformed. Again, ironically, something from the New World would trigger that change. It was not an invention but a tiny aphid that was to devastate the vineyards of France.

Like greenfly, the aphid phylloxera lives by sucking sap out of plant stems, in this case vines. When sucking, it injects tiny quantities of saliva into the plant and, just as an *Anopheles* mosquito bite might give a human being malaria, a non-immune vines infected with phylloxera withered and died. American vines were impervious to this, but not French ones. Phylloxera somehow got to France –

with catastrophic results. Accurate figures are not available but it is reckoned that between a third and a half of France's vineyards were wiped out. Among the worst-hit were those of Cognac and the Charente, the heartland of brandy output. Britain's brandy tipplers found their favourite hooch was no longer available – except at prices only the very rich could look at. In due course, French vineyards were restored – largely by planting or grafting immune US vines. But for several years in the 1870s, brandy was not available. The English brandy-drinking classes, *faute de mieux*, switched to Scotch.

Fortuitously, another increasingly popular drink in Britain at that time was Spain's great fortified wine, 'Xeres' – anglified into 'sherry' – which came to Britain in large casks. Returning the empty ones to Spain was simply not viable, so large numbers of good but redundant sherry butts became available in London and other ports of arrival. Although most Scots distilleries employed coopers to make their own barrels, the thrifty distillers saw these sherry casks as a bargain too good to miss. And so they were. By coastal steamer or by rail, they were shipped to Scotland and, after repairs, pressed into use. The whisky matured in them soaked up something of the remaining essences of the sherry still held within the wood.

A lot of whisky thus matured tasted passably like brandy. Many brandy drinkers who, despite initial reluctance, switched to whisky enjoyed the new spirit and stuck with it, even after brandy returned to the market some years later.

About that time, another welcome arrival on the scene was the mass-produced glass bottle. We take glass bottles utterly for granted today – indeed they are now being supplanted by cheaper plastic containers – but until the last quarter of the 19th century, bottles of standard size, quality and durability hardly existed. They were hand-blown and tended to vary slightly in size and shape. Also, many were round-bottomed and would not stand upright unless a special cradle was provided, not unlike the raffia jacket of Chianti bottles. However, the development of better blowing and moulding techniques raised quality and lowered unit prices. Bulk bottling became a viable if labour-intensive proposition, but for some years to come, casked whisky remained cheaper than bottled whisky, especially in Scotland.

Finally, there came blending. Like all good ideas, it seems so obvious and one almost wonders why it took so long to arrive. The answer lies in part in the fragmentation of the whisky industry. Each distillery made its own whisky, malt or grain, and sold it by the barrel to its own customers. It made sense by the norms of the time. Until the late 19th century, the concept of a branded product sold throughout the UK had yet to come of age. One very simple test proves this: read a gazetteer or guidebook to any medium-size Scots town in the late Victorian era and it will probably list a gasworks, some bakeries, a brewery or two, a town savings bank and, possibly, a small distillery. Such a list is unthinkable today. There would be no breweries, no local savings bank, no gasworks and just two or three bakers facing ever-greater competition from the supermarkets selling mass-produced bread.

However, the growth of the whisky industry had created a new animal – the whisky and spirit merchant, who bought, sold and distributed whisky and other drinks in bulk throughout Britain and often overseas. Many were aware of whisky's shortcomings and idiosyncrasies. Grain whiskies were smooth but dull. Malts had flavour and charisma, but varied from batch to batch. The solution was blended whisky which combined grain and malt and ironed out their inconsistencies to give a consistently good drink. Furthermore, such whisky could now be bottled and brand-labelled – a breakthrough generally attributed to Andrew Usher.

True, compared to the great shipyards, railway workshops and engineering works of the late Victorian era, the whisky industry was still relatively minor, but in terms of geographical diversity and exports, it could hold its head high. The proof lies in the peripatetic Alfred Barnard's marvellous book *The Whisky Distilleries of the United Kingdom*, published in 1887. In that decade there were almost 160 UK distilleries producing whisky. Scotland had 129 (including 21 in Campbeltown alone). Ireland, still part of the UK then, had 28 and England had four. And, in the years between Barnard's grand tour and the year 1900, another two dozen were to be built.

The success and vitality of the industry seemed boundless. Thanks to increasing productivity, static taxation and excise duties and good transport links, spirits were cheap and universally available as never before. Yet had Alfred Barnard repeated his tour 40 years later, he would have found a blighted, decimated and despairing industry. What went wrong?

Temperance and David Lloyd George

In the last decades of the 19th century, Britain stood at what historians regard as the pinnacle of its powers. British industry was the envy of the world, the Royal Navy ruled the waves and a vast area of the school globe in every classroom was coloured an indiscreet pink to show it was part of the British Empire. In addition, Britain was a country of cheap drink. In pubs and ale-houses, a gill of whisky (one third of a pint) cost as little as fourpence, and the whisky would have been far stronger than the 40% alcohol by volume which is standard today. That, in a way, was the problem. It was too cheap and, in an era when many people faced great poverty, bad housing, overcrowding, poor sanitation and other social evils, drink was the one solace.

Charles Dickens portrayed much of the drudgery of life at that time just as George Bernard Shaw did two generations later. Both dramatised the woes of the poor, particularly the fact that alcohol and drunkenness exacerbated those problems. Alcoholism was rife, in some areas almost out of control. A scan of the local papers of the time in most regions of Britain quickly unearths numerous court reports dealing solely with drunkenness. This example from the *Partick and Maryhill Press* of 12 May 1894 is typical.

> *Robert Dewart, a cordwainer, hailing from Glasgow, pled guilty of conducting himself in a disorderly manner on the north bank of the Clyde in the vicinity of Meadowside shipbuilding yard on Sunday last, and attempting to go into the river. The poor man was the worse for drink, and was inconsolable because all the pubs were closed, therefore he proposed to end his troubles with a big drink of Clyde water. He was fined 7/6d or five days imprisonment.*

By the turn of the century the churches, women's groups and the temperance movement all targeted drink as the root of society's evils. It was not strictly accurate – any more than it is right to blame car makers for all car accidents – but there was no doubt many people saw alcohol as a great blight upon society.

Temperance rallies, exhortations from a thousand pulpits and other steps were tried to stem the tide, all to little avail. Then in 1909 the Chancellor of the Exchequer, David Lloyd George, did the unthinkable. He raised the tax on spirits to the unheard of level of 15 shillings a proof gallon. Topers choked when they saw the new prices chalked up in their locals and demand dropped like a stone.

Although Lloyd George's tax hike had a sobering effect on the populace, it did little to fatten the Exchequer – the drop in demand far outweighed the extra revenue. But it set an awesome precedent, prompting the excise duty on spirits to be raised sixfold in the ensuing 11 years.

With the outbreak of World War I, another indignity was to hit the licensed trade. Output from munitions factories lagged badly in the winter of 1914-15, at a time when every shell and bullet was badly needed. The cause was largely lack of raw materials and poor management. However, the government saw drink as the culprit. Public house opening hours were drastically curtailed – two or three hours at lunch-time and four hours or so at night became the norm, with closure by 10pm at the latest. The strength of spirits was sharply reduced, especially in areas around military bases or munitions works. These measures were declared as temporary for the duration of the conflict, but were to endure for nigh on 70 years – an interesting comment on the political inertia of the British.

From the whisky distillers' point of view there were the more serious Government curbs on supplies of barley for malt distilling although these were understandable at a time when every ounce was needed to feed the war effort. However, the grain distillers were less affected. Industrial alcohol was needed in great quantities for manufacturing and solvent purposes and fusel oil was needed to make varnishes and aircraft 'dope'.

Several distilleries had already closed in the early years of the century as late-Victorian boom turned into Edwardian slump. More closed in the aftermath of the 1909 duty rise. Many surviving distilleries were 'mothballed' for the duration of the war. The producers remained unconcerned as the tide of war moved Britain's way, believing that once it was over things were bound to improve. With that in mind, there was a big rush back into production in 1919. Their optimism was to be severely dented. The 1920s were to prove the darkest era yet for the industry.

Several factors caused the downward spiral of the 1920s. US prohibition hit the industry's main export market although large quantities of Scotch continued to reach the American market for 'medicinal purposes' and via the bootleggers. The US decline could not be offset by better home sales. Whisky had been hit by more swingeing excise duty increases, coupled with statutory price controls. These meant the industry could only pass on half the increase to the public, who still balked at the post-war set price of 12 shillings a bottle. Lastly, an austere, temperate mood now gripped Britain. Whisky and high spirits were definitely out of fashion. Scotland even held a national referendum on prohibition in December 1920. Although the nation voted staunchly to keep the dram, the very fact a referendum was held at all indicated how powerful the temperance movement had become. The grim decade dragged on through the 1926 General Strike, the 1929 Wall Street crash to the Great Depression of 1930-34. At one brief point in the early 1930s, there were only eight functioning distilleries left in Scotland. Ireland, as the so-called Irish Free State after 1922, fared even worse: its tally dropped from 28 to just two.

The Scotch industry might well have gone into irrevocable decline but for the vision, determination and resolve of one man: William Ross, the general manager and later chairman of the Distillers Company Ltd. His portrait reveals a thin-faced, gaunt man with a Calvinist bearing, piercing eyes and a short pointed beard. Ross proved to be the saviour of the industry, but he did it at great cost by buying out and shutting down innumerable distilleries and urging or obliging the competition to do the same. Yet he was no ruthless butcher or self-glorifying tycoon. Even rivals and competitors admired his fairness and honesty. His vision of DCL was a combine 'strong enough to withstand the temptation to crush a weaker competitor who is striving by legitimate means to make an honest livelihood, yet strong enough to keep unscrupulous competitors in check.' Such integrity earned him the reputation of 'the Abraham Lincoln of the trade', one which he was to dominate from 1897 until 1935 during which time he made DCL the supreme giant of the whisky industry.

The lion's share of distillery closures stem from his era, though some were to reopen as the industry boomed in the new golden era following World War II. The closures were widely spread, from the Borders to Orkney, from the Isles to the Lowlands. Worst hit of all was Campbeltown, where 18 of its 21 distilleries folded, nearly all of them in the 1920s. An additional factor here was the exhaustion of Drumlemble colliery near Machrihanish which had provided cheap local coal to the distilleries for 200 years. The pit closure also proved the death knell for the narrow-guage railway that brought the coal to Campbeltown, though it struggled on as a summer tourist attraction until the early 1930s, a sad remnant and an unfitting reminder of the glory days.

EXPANSION AND PROSPERITY

The upturn of the industry came in 1934 with a modest economic revival in the UK and the scrapping of prohibition in the US by President Franklin D. Roosevelt. Neither event made much difference in the short term, but they restored enough confidence to prompt widespread resumption of distilling with an eye to a better future. That came quickly. By 1938 output has soared to 38 million gallons, the highest since the turn of the century.

World War II caused wild fluctuations in the fortunes of the whisky industry. It was initially directed to maintain, even increase, exports to the US to pay for Britain's vast purchases of raw materials and war-effort equipment. Once Lend-Lease came in, the pressure for such whisky exports dropped, but US-bound exports were maintained throughout the conflict. As in World War I, the need to preserve cereals for human and livestock consumption drastically curtailed supplies for distilling. Again almost all distilleries were mothballed and virtually no whisky at all was distilled in 1943. As the war neared its end, however, Churchill penned his famous memo stating that distilling should restart since it was a key export earner. As a result, 30 distilleries reopened for business in January 1945.

The post-war Labour government, either by accident or design, made life very tough for the industry. Again the emphasis was on exports, with home-market sales tightly controlled at a fraction of export sales. At one point this ratio dropped to 20 per cent, meaning a company had to export four cases for every case it was allowed to sell on the UK market. This led to great problems for producers and publicans and to a brief but thriving black market.

It was not until the late 1950s that the whisky industry finally shook off the aftermath of the war. Simultaneously, it found there was now a truly global thirst for Scotch which the existing portfolio of distilleries could not hope to meet. For the first time in the 20th century, a big building programme of new distilleries got under way, matched by a parallel programme of restoring and re-equipping older distilleries, many of which had not burned a peat in anger for 50 years.

Something like two dozen abandoned distilleries were given the kiss of life. Some were still in a reasonable state of repair. Others – such as the Craighouse Distillery on Jura – had sunk into dereliction and ruin. No matter: it and many others were restored and living smoke again spiralled from their chimneys.

For nearly 25 years after 1957, the industry enjoyed its greatest-ever boom. Output, exports, home sales, bulk exports, volume and value of stocks, all rose consistently. For the first time, a global market developed for single-malts, thanks to Glen Grant's remarkable penetration of the Italian market and William Grant's tour de force with Glenfiddich. There were problems however – ever-increasing UK duties for one and discriminatory taxation against Scotch by countries keen to protect their indigenous spirit distillers. But worries were few and far between. There was occasional over-production and overstocking – always a problem for an industry with several years time lag between initial production and final sale – but it hardly ever lead to anything more than a slightly extended traditional 'silent season'.

Not until the early 1980s was a downturn serious enough to cause distillery closures. In 1983 DCL closed 11 malt distilleries as other producers mothballed a number of their distilleries as well. As the late-1980s economic boom progressed, a handful were reopened – a move that may have been sadly premature. As the recession of the early 1990s gained impetus, it initially looked as if Scotch would weather the storm but declining sales and excess bonded stocks finally claimed its first victims. In February 1993, United Malt & Grain Distillers (the distilling arm of United Distillers, the new banner for DCL and Arthur Bell & Sons Ltd since the Guinness takeovers of the mid-1980s) announced the closure of four distilleries: Bladnoch near Wigtown (Scotland's most southerly distillery), Balmenach at Cromdale, Pittyvaich at Dufftown and Rosebank at Falkirk. UD also announced the phasing out of all their grain distilleries bar Port Dundas in Glasgow and Cameron Bridge in Fife.

Several other permanent closures were announced in the early to mid-1990s, including Allied Domecq's Lochside Distillery in Montrose, Morrison Bowmore Distillers' Glengarioch Distillery at Oldmeldrum and a handful of distilleries which had stood idle since they were mothballed in the 1980s. All of these distilleries are covered in part two of this book.

However, the darkest hour seems to have passed and prospects for the industry are bright, especially after Japan's move to end discriminatory taxation on Scotch and signs of a gradual change to standardise duty on spirits within the EU. The Scotch Whisky Association continues to lobby vigorously on behalf of its members in order to persuade the government that Scotch must be subject to a fairer tax within the EU if it is to thrive. The enduring excellence of the product and distilling's growing importance to the tourist industry are also strong points. Sceptics may dismiss distilleries as factories churning out alcohol – but many Scots distilleries now vie with castles and stately homes as Scotland's leading tourist attractions. Some of them attract over 100,000 visitors per annum. And there are few factories in any industry in any country which can make a claim like that.

THE NORTH

Although the Highlands were the focal area for illicit distilling before the Excise Act of 1823 – and the last holdout of such activity for decades afterwards – there have been surprisingly few distilleries, in proportion to population, built around and north of Inverness. The one exception was Orkney, where until the late 1920s there were three distilleries, two of which are still going strong today. On the other hand, the combined counties of Caithness and Sutherland have never had more than three official distilleries operating at any one time, all of which are or were close to the East coast. Today, one (Pulteney) is in Wick while two are in Brora. These are Clynelish, built between 1967-68 by Scottish Malt Distillers as an addition to a smaller distillery (also named Clynelish), founded in 1819. The old Clynelish distillery was renamed Brora after 1969 and stayed in production until about 1983, when it was mothballed and it is now a lost distillery.

Easter Ross has fared considerably better. It has about half a dozen in operation today, including the giant grain complex at Invergordon, now part of Whyte and Mackay, plus such noted names as Dalmore, Glenmorangie, Ord, Balblair and Teaninich.

In its heyday Inverness had three distilleries, not one of which survives today. In all, the lost distillery tally for the North now stands at ten, namely:

Ben Wyvis (*aka* Ferintosh), Dingwall (1879-1926)

Gerston, Halkirk, Caithness (1798-1882)

Gerston II (*aka* Ben Morven), Halkirk (1886-1911)

Glen Albyn, Inverness (1846-1986)

Glen Mhor, Inverness (1892-1986)

Glenskiach, Evanton, Easter Ross (1896-1926)

Man O' Hoy, (*aka* Stromness), Orkney (1817-1928)

Millburn, (*aka* Inverness) (1807-1988)

Old Clynelish/Brora, Brora, Sutherland (1819-1983)

Pollo, Delny, Easter Ross (1817-1903)

BEN WYVIS, *Dingwall*

The lands of Ferintosh near Dingwall have two claims to fame. They were mentioned several times by the Brahan Seer, the great Highland mystic with the gift of 'second sight', and they enjoyed a near unique position in the history of whisky making. In 1689 the laird, Duncan Forbes of Culloden, had his lands sacked by the Jacobites for supporting King William of Orange. In recompense, he was allowed to distil and sell whisky free of duty for an annual fee of 400 Scottish merks. It was a privilege amply exploited for several generations with four or more distilleries operating at Ferintosh in the 18th century. Ultimately the privilege was withdrawn due to unfair commercial advantage Ferintosh whisky enjoyed. Its reputation was considerable and its demise moved Robert Burns to lament its going.

But the only major industrial distillery to operate near Ferintosh was Ben Wyvis. It was built in 1879, cut into a steep hillock close to the Cromarty Firth, with the railway line and main road to Dingwall running between distillery and shore. For its time it was big with an annual output of 160,000 gallons and its own rail sidings. A local water source was not available so a pipeline was run four miles up to Loch Ussie – into whose waters, one legend has it, the Brahan Seer threw his wondrous 'stone of vision' when he was condemned to death.

Alfred Barnard described the distillery in 1887 with awe. It was very advanced with vast malting floors, large conveyor belts and hoppers, a powerful horizontal steam engine and ingenious systems for recycling heat. It embodied ideas well ahead of its time – not only could farmers buy draff, but also pot ale from a special tank. Other equipment included four 13,000-gallon washbacks and a 4,000-gallon wash still.

The former bonded warehouse of Ben Wyvis

Despite this fine array of capital equipment, the distillery had a sadly chequered history. It was sold in 1887 to Scotch Whisky Distillers Ltd, who were wound up barely two years later. It was then acquired by a Belfast firm in 1893, who renamed it Ferintosh and ran it successfully for 20 years. Control of Ferintosh passed to the Belfast division of Distillers Finance Corporation in 1914, which in turn was bought out by DCL in 1922.

DCL liquidated the Ferintosh Company in 1924, transferring the licence to its subsidiary, John Begg Ltd. However, things did not improve and the distillery was closed in 1926. The buildings gradually fell into decay and ruin, although the warehouses were used by Scottish Malt Distillers until the early 1980s. Today the trackside warehouses are still standing, with their own rail siding and the stores and office building are now a business centre. The hilltop granaries and maltbarns are semi-demolished.

But the Ben Wyvis name did not pass away completely. In 1965, Invergordon Distillers chose the name for a new malt distillery within their Invergordon grain complex. That distillery too has been indefinitely shut down but it is perhaps not impossible that the name Ben Wyvis may be used again.

GERSTON, *Halkirk*

Gerston distillery was first registered by one Francis Swanson in 1796 near a farm of the same name on the banks of the Thurso River close to Halkirk. It was an area noted at the time for its numerous illicit distillers. The business stayed small until 1825 when two sons, John and James Swanson, expanded the business and pushed their whisky to a wider market.

Although the family firm had mixed fortunes it closed from 1851-52 and was subsequently run by James Swanson, the whisky gained a remarkably wide reputation. Its fame spread to London and among its devotees were many politicians, including Sir Robert Peel, Prime Minister from 1841-46 and creator of the police. However, such fame did not ensure the immortality of the company. The Swanson family sold the distillery in 1872, possibly after the death of James Swanson, and the unrecorded new owners failed to make a go of things. It finally closed in 1875 and was demolished by 1882. Nothing remains of the distillery except some piles of stone and rubble and a low wall 300 yards upriver from Gerston Farm. However, it is reported that the Loch Dubh Hotel in Caithness possesses one virgin bottle of the Gerston malt.

GERSTON II, *Halkirk*

The closure of Gerston and loss of its fine spirit caused more than a few lamentations in London, where it had a strong following. This prompted a London company to build a second distillery close by between Gerston Farm and Halkirk Bridge in 1886-87. The operators called themselves the Gerston Distillery Company and acquired rights to tap the Calder Burn the water source used by the first distillery.

On completion, Gerston II was the most visible landmark for miles around in the bleak countryside near Halkirk and Georgemas rail junction. One of its early employees was young William Grant junior, second son of William Grant of Glenfiddich, who was employed as a bookkeeper. Shortly before he was due to return to join the family firm on Speyside in 1888, he tragically died of typhoid fever. On a more positive note, an early visitor was the ubiquitous Alfred Barnard in 1886. He waxed eloquent about the skillful construction and layout of the new distillery which was then among the first to use only one boiler to steam-heat all the stills and supply hot water for the mash tun.

Despite its design excellence and a facility to double output from 80,000 to 160,000 gallons a year if need be, the new distillery lacked the Swanson's magic touch. Its whisky not only failed to tempt the palates of its intended London clientele but also failed to make enough money and was sold in 1897 to Northern Distilleries Ltd. They renamed it Ben Morven after the hill viewed from the distillery on the southern horizon.

Its history over the next few years is obscure. One good source states the new company was wound up in 1900 and the distillery closed. But a picture exists from the Edwardian era showing the workforce of 18 lined up beside the bowler-hatted manager and his wife. A local press story says the distillery closed in 1911, while a historic review of Caithness industry said it finally closed at the start of World War I.

The buildings were demolished in stages, the high chimney coming down in 1918. The stillhouse was recently said to be still standing and the tunnel aqueduct sluice gates on the Calder Burn which supplied the distillery are also still there. In addition, several houses linked to Ben Morven are lived in today, but as separate private residences. The great dream of repeating the Gerston success came, alas, to nothing.

GLEN ALBYN, *Inverness*

By the mid-1840s, the great spate of closures after the 'gold rush' of the 1820s had subsided and demand for whisky was at last starting to exceed supply. Several distilleries were started about that time in the North, of which Glen Albyn was to prove a long-term survivor. Founded by Inverness Provost James Sutherland, it was built beside the Caledonian Canal basin on the site of a ruined brewery and was formally inaugurated on 10 October 1844.

Like most distilleries in this book, it had an up-and-down existence. It was badly damaged by fire in November 1849, though it was distilling again by February 1850. Within five years it had fallen on hard times and was put up for sale. No buyer was interested and it was converted to a flour mill in 1866 after years of disuse. However, it was rebuilt as a distillery in 1884 by Gregory (or Grigor) and Company, with an estimated annual output of 75,000 gallons.

Glen Albyn Distillery, 1974 (John R.Hume)

Alfred Barnard visited it two years later and noted two pot stills, a wash still and a low-wines still. The distillery had two notable features for the time: the worm pipes from the stills were not circular in section but shaped like a capital D with the flat side down. This, it was claimed, cooled the spirit quicker and improved the flavour. Also, the distillery was linked to its head office a mile away by telephone.

It went through a couple of name changes – Glenalbyn Distillery Co, 1891-3, to which 'Ltd' was added in 1895. In 1892 it had a near neighbour constructed, Glen Mhor, a venture led by Glen Albyn manager John Birnie and James Mackinlay of Leith blenders Charles Mackinlay and Co. Glen Albyn was eventually bought over in 1920 by the Glen Mhor operators Mackinlays and Birnie Ltd. They in turn were bought out by DCL in 1972 and Glen Albyn was eventually transferred to Scottish Malt Distillers (SMD).

Its more recent history is not extensively documented. With Glen Mhor it installed Saladin maltings in 1954, among the first in Scotland. These were used until the early 1980s. Down the years Glen Albyn tended to be overshadowed by Glen Mhor, especially as the latter's whisky seemed to have an 'edge' in both flavour and popularity over its own spirit. Output, which peaked at 320,000 gallons a year in postwar times, almost wholly went for blending.

Glen Albyn was among a sheaf of distilleries mothballed by DCL and SMD in the early 1980s. It was closed in 1983 and was one of several that was never to reopen. It was finally demolished in 1986 and the site developed for a supermarket.

GLEN MHOR, *Inverness*

Glen Mhor (pronounced Vawr) was launched in 1892 as Glen Albyn's immediate neighbour and was also sandwiched between the Caledonian Canal basin and the River Ness. It was conveniently close to a rail spur from the Highland Line, giving it unrivalled rail and water transport access. Interestingly, plans for a 'new distillery' at Muirtown were recorded as being approved by Inverness Dean of Guild Court in January 1896, with the plant duly opened in October that year. Whether there was a four year lapse between launch and construction, or whether the 1896 approval was for an extension to Glen Mhor is not clear.

During its early decades it was managed by John Birnie, ex-Glen Albyn, who seems to have been the proverbial man for all seasons – a good manager and businessman, a great character and (like Glen Albyn's founder, James Sutherland) a provost of Inverness. Whisky was very much in the Birnie family blood and his son, William, was involved with Glen Mhor for many years as well. William died in his eighties in 1973, a year after DCL had wholly taken over both distilleries.

In addition to the remarkable repute of its whisky, Glen Mhor had one other claim to fame. The noted Highland novelist and whisky writer, Neil Gunn, spent his younger years there as an exciseman. Decades later, he retired to a house across the Beauly Firth,

Glen Mhor Distillery, 1936 (Highland Folk Museum, Kingussie)

almost within sight of the distillery. He remained a devotee of Glen Mhor to his last days and admitted as much in his famous epigram: 'Until a man has had the luck to chance upon a perfectly matured malt, he does not really know what whisky is.' This was written with Glen Mhor in mind. Another devotee with a polished turn of phrase said Glen Mhor had 'an honest subtle richness and "fatness" reminiscent of the patina of old furniture.'

Its quality accounts for the fact that Mackinlays sold Glen Mhor as a single malt even when blends utterly dominated the market and it was an important constituent of many leading blends.

For decades its fortunes and fate seemed inextricably linked to Glen Albyn. It too installed Saladin maltings around 1954, was bought out by DCL in 1972, mothballed in 1983 and was eventually closed and demolished in 1986. Occasionally, rare bottles of Glen Mhor turn up on dark back shelves of old grocers' shops and off-licences. They are well worth buying, mainly to ascertain the truth of Neil Gunn's eloquent lines and certainly not to be used as furniture polish.

GLENSKIACH, *Evanton, Easter Ross*

The western edge of the Cromarty Firth has had its fair share of distilleries, of which four are thriving names today. Glenskiach did well enough in its time, yet mysteriously went into voluntary liquidation in May 1926 at the time of the General Strike.

It was established in September 1896, with capital of 18,000. The instigator was John Ross of Evanton, who became its company secretary and general manager. He was backed by London wine merchants and a several local worthies. The distillery was to be built on the River Skiach (or Skiack) which flows south of Evanton into the Cromarty Firth. Construction contracts were awarded in October of that year, though exactly when distilling started is not recorded.

The distillery had a lot going for it. It was well situated, the river was a good water source, the railway was close at hand and small cargo boats could bring barley, coal and peat to a nearby landing stage. John Ross had an excellent distilling pedigree; his father Andrew was distiller at Balblair and his uncle, James Munro, had the Pollo distillery at Delny, up the coast on the Dornoch Firth. It is known that John Ross remained manager throughout Glenskiach's existence.

Glenskiach Distillery, c1900

Glenskiach went through a tough period between 1908-10, when it had to borrow extensively, but 1910 saw its last recorded loss of £307. It stayed open through the difficult years of World War I, probably thanks to the proximity of the Invergordon and Scapa naval bases, and made a record profit of £4720 in 1920. Profits fell gradually during the ensuing years – they were down to £1852 in 1925 – but that does not explain why, apparently without warning, the directors voted to wind up the company in 1926 with the final board meeting being held in November 1932.

Employees and locals mourned the loss. 'It was a good distillery. I don't know why they knocked it down – it was a better-built distillery than either Teaninich or Dalmore', said one local, Duncan Fraser. 'But then 1926 was a slack time.'

Alex Campbell of Braegowan recalls how when the pot ale was disgorged into the Skiach, the river foamed and frothed for hours and badly affected the fish – though he also said it made the ducks pretty frisky!

The distillery was damaged by a bad fire in 1929 and was demolished in 1933, the fall of its high chimney attracting crowds from miles around. Stone from the buildings was used to build a new bridge across the River Averon on the Struie Road. The various distillery houses and cottages were sold to their occupants. The distillery office, with its delightful clock under the gable was converted into a house. None of the occupants have reported any finds of hidden bottles, although Janet Parkin, who lived in the brewer's cottage, said her kitchen smelled strongly of whisky as late as the 1970s. The dwellings and considerable remnants of the half-mile long mill lade are virtually all that remain today of Glenskiach, the distillery that sadly went down with the General Strike.

MAN O'HOY, *Stromness, Orkney*

Of all Scotland's offshore islands, Orkney is the most agrarian. Despite the raw North Atlantic gales that tear across it and the Pentland Firth, the islands enjoy a relatively mild climate, ample rainfall and fertile soil. Certain cereals grow well, livestock thrives and the islands largely escaped the turmoil and bloodshed that all too often ravaged the Highlands.

It is not unsurprising, therefore, to find that Orkney has a good distilling pedigree with two remaining distilleries in operation today. Kirkwall's Highland Park first opened in 1795 and in the mid-1820s some five or six legal distilleries were registered in and around the town, doubtless with many more illicit ones elsewhere in the parish. Few of these early distilleries survived more than a decade. The other survivor is Scapa, near Kirkwall, but it was a late arrival, being built in 1885 and only escaped terminal fire damage during World War I thanks to prompt assistance from the Royal Navy in Scapa Flow.

But Orkney laments one 20th century loss – Man O'Hoy Distillery at Stromness. It stood only yards from the dark waters of Stromness harbour opposite the Inner and Outer Holms and Scapa Flow. As it was a small community where zoning was unheard of, only a narrow alley separated it from the town hall – and the town hall was built 40 years after the distillery. It came into operation in 1817 under one John Crookshanks and within 40 years had no fewer than six different owners or operators. Alfred Barnard, however, reported the distillery as opened in 1828 by one Hector Munn. Whatever the case, it seems it was initially known as Stromness distillery, its whisky as Man O'Hoy.

In the mid-1860s it fell into disuse. It was bought in 1878 by the Macpherson Brothers who restored and ran it until the turn of the century. They are thought to have renamed the distillery Man O'Hoy and the whisky Old Orkney, though it was better known by its initials O.O. Output was small: in the 1880s and 1890s it was about 7,000 gallons a year, making it the tiniest and most isolated Scottish distillery of its era.

Like many early distilleries it was built on a steep site, so the liquid flow from mash tun to underback to washback to stills was gravity-driven without help from pumps. All water came from the May Burn, which streamed past from its source below Black Craig. The May Burn also turned a nine foot water wheel which powered the malt mill, though by the mid-1880s a 12hp steam engine did much of that task. The entire operation was carried out within the one narrow edifice, built on top of a once-clandestine vault used by illicit distillers. The only separate buildings were two warehouses which sheltered about 300 casks.

Between 1900 and 1910 it was acquired by J&J McConnell Ltd, Belfast, with the distillery becoming a separate London registered company, McConnells Distillery Ltd. Like all too many others, it succumbed to the bad times of the 1920s. It was silent from 1928 and was wound up and demolished in 1940. A new housing scheme occupies the site, adhering closely to the outline of the distillery. The May Burn is now safely, if sadly culverted.

This bottle from Stromness Distillery fetched £1045 at auction in Nov 1992
(Courtesy of Christie's, Glasgow)

MILLBURN, *Inverness*

Millburn is by far the oldest distillery in Inverness and, by some quirk of fate, the only one still standing – though it is now a steak-house restaurant. However, today's building is almost certainly not the original but stems from the distillery's extension and reconstruction in 1876.

It has had a very varied existence that could justify a small book rather than the synopsis given here. It was built a mile from town, just off the main Elgin road and under the sheer brow of a hill beside the Mill Burn, which supplied cooling water and gave it its name. Process water was brought – though not necessarily when the distillery was first built – eight miles by pipeline from Loch Duntelchaig. It was originally established around 1805-7 by a Mr Welsh, petered into obscurity for 20 years, then was licensed in 1825 to Messrs Rose and Macdonald. Their company was dissolved in 1829. Over the next decade it was sold or leased to no fewer than

Millburn Distillery, 1959

three different operators, was defunct by 1851 and acquired around 1853 by David Rose, a corn merchant, probably for use as a mill. Certainly, it was not registered as a distillery for more than 20 years.

It was rebuilt as a distillery in 1876 and within two years had built up sufficient repute to win an order to send a large whisky consignment to the British garrison on Cyprus. In 1881 Mr Rose's son, George, took over and it was he who welcomed Alfred Barnard when he visited five years later. In 1892 it was bought by the Andrew Haig organisation and the company was renamed the Millburn Distillery Co in 1904. In 1921 Millburn was acquired by Booth's, of London Gin fame, who were to see it burn down shortly after they bought it. It was rebuilt in 1922 and, despite the struggle of the years between the wars, it kept going with only occasional downtime until it was acquired by DCL in 1943.

DCL operated it until the early 1980s downturn, which led to its closure in early 1985. It was bought by the Beefeater restaurant chain around 1990 and is now a steakhouse operating under the name 'The Auld Distillery'.

It could be argued that Millburn had ceased to be viable with the arrival of the new, custom-built automated distilleries of the 1970s and 1980s. It was on a small cramped sight at Diriebught, hemmed in on virtually all sides by steep hill, road and river. Expansion was not possible and, with the growth of Inverness, it sat in an urban rather than semi-rural setting. Its whisky, although good, was relatively obscure as a single malt. Its equipment and outbuildings were also outdated and too small. Its closure in hindsight was inevitable. However, its use as a steakhouse has allowed many features of the distillery to be retained, as well as its historic link with Highland hospitality. Amid the many sadder stories to follow in this book, one has to admit that Millburn's has had a relatively happy ending.

OLD CLYNELISH/BRORA, *Brora*

Clynelish was, and is, a very successful distillery producing one of the most enduring single malts which has a great following among both blenders and single malt enthusiasts. It was started by the Marquis of Stafford, later to be the first Duke of Sutherland, in 1819 to provide a local outlet for cereals grown on Brora allotments kept by inland crofters displaced during the Clearances. It also provided

The Old Clynelish Distillery or Brora Distillery, c 1880

employment and legal spirit to compete against that from local illicit distillers. A nearby coal seam, mined since the 16th century, provided cheap fuel (though Fife coal was later shipped in) and several local peat bogs provided fuel for the kiln.

The distillery had operated for four years when the 1823 Act gave legal distilling the green light. In theory, Clynelish should have thrived from then on. In reality, the licencees sometimes had an uphill struggle. First of these was James Harper, from Midlothian (1825-27 and 1828-34). Then came Andrew Ross (1834-46) and then George Lawson who, with his sons, was to run the distillery for 50 years. In 1896 the Glasgow blenders James Ainslie bought and rebuilt Clynelish.

After Ainslie's went bankrupt in 1912, the distillery was bought by a limited company jointly owned by DCL and the Risk family, with the John Walker company taking some equity in 1916. In 1930, DCL took over full ownership, transferred the distillery to SMD and mothballed it from 1931-39. It ticked over quietly in the war years and thrived in the postwar era. Demand eventually outgrew its production capacity. To meet this, work started in 1967 on a new distillery nearby, which opened in 1969. The new plant was given the name Clynelish and the old distillery renamed Brora. Both distilleries functioned in tandem for 14 years but in 1983 Brora was indefinitely mothballed by DCL with more than a dozen others.

When Barnard visited it in 1886, he described a thriving but small establishment standing on a two-acre site of stone-walled and slate-roofed buildings set in a quadrangle. There were three granaries holding in all about 500 tons of barley, two malt barns (one with a stone steep, the other iron) and a peat-burning kiln holding five tons at a time. The shallow mash tun was 13 feet across and the worts passed via underback and coolers to four small washbacks holding 3,000 gallons each.

The still house had two pot stills, then almost new, of unrecorded capacity, plus the usual wash and low-wines chargers and receivers for low wines and spirits. The casking store vat held 900 gallons and the five warehouses held 900 puncheons of whisky. Output, due in part to a long summer silent season, was a modest 20,000 gallons a year. Process water was brought from a nearby stream in iron pipes and all machinery was powered by a large overshot water wheel. Such was the whisky's repute that, unusually, the distillery supplied only private customers and had ceased accepting trade orders!

Since the distillery was closed in 1983, neither DCL nor its successor, United Distillers, have given any indication that they will restore or reopen Brora, a situation that shows no sign of altering as the industry seeks to create larger, more efficient malt distilleries. Although it is still standing and thought to be largely complete, Brora is definitely now a lost distillery.

POLLO, *Delny*

Information on this distillery is as hard to come by as bottles of single malts from most of the distilleries in this book. This was a small, farm-based establishment largely linked to the Ross family who had strong connections to the nearby Balblair Distillery. It first opened in 1817 with Mr W.B. Rose named as the distiller, but it closed in 1821. In 1825 John Ross from Balblair brought Pollo back to life, but that venture lasted barely a year.

For 70 years after 1826 the distillery lay idle, though it was probably converted to be used as a mill within the farm complex. Then in 1896 Andrew Ross of Balblair re-established Pollo as a distillery, though he remained at Balblair and put his brother-in-law, James Munro, in to manage Pollo. About that time John Ross (who was probably Andrew's son) became manager at the newly-built

Glenskiach, some miles to the south. The Rosses were a distilling power to be reckoned with in the area, but despite this, Pollo never enjoyed great success and closed again in 1903 and has not been used as a distillery since. The farm itself and some of the buildings that probably housed the distillery are still standing today.

Speyside And The North-East

Since 1950, Speyside has become the powerful heart of the Scotch malt distilling industry, inexorably overtaking Islay and long-eclipsed Campbeltown. There are relatively few wholly 'lost distilleries' in and around Speyside and more than two dozen new distilleries have been built there since World War II. However, Speyside has known bad times and, as the main malt distilling area, its scattered small communities have often been hard-hit by the vicissitudes of the industry. At various times, up to 20 distilleries have been mothballed, with some standing idle for up to 50 or 60 years in all, or for much of the time they have stood on Moray or Banffshire soil.

A growing problem facing Speyside malt distilleries is that, with ownership passing to evermore remote hands, decisions on whether they stay open, or are mothballed or irrevocably shut are no longer taken in Scotland. Decisions are taken in London or even further afield. With whisky a global industry, market changes in, say, Japan or Australia can affect demand for a particular malt, leading to the closure of one distillery with dire consequences for the locality where it may be virtually the sole employer.

Mothballings or closures during the 1980s included Imperial at Carron, Glentauchers at Mulben, Royal Brackla at Cawdor, Balmenach near Cromdale, Benromach at Forres and Mannochmore near Elgin. By the 1990s, those six and others were either back in part-time or full production or being prepared for restart under new ownership. The 1990s also saw a raft of distilleries changing hands, the most notable being the sale of Macallan-Glenlivet.

Two malt distilleries which 'disappeared' during this period, Mosstowie and Glencraig, were not quite the losses they seemed.

Both were annexes of other distilleries and used Lomond-type stills to produce a different-tasting spirit. Mosstowie was added to Miltonduff-Glenlivet in 1974, Glencraig to Glenburgie at Alves in 1958. In recent years both have been phased out, though their distinctive malts can still be ordered from specialist bottlers.

Also, there are two distilleries which, despite much pondering, I feel cannot yet be listed as 'lost': Dallas Dhu and Pittyvaich.

Lying two miles south of Forres, Dallas Dhu was built in 1899, was badly hit by fire in 1939, closed by DCL in 1983 and donated in 1986 by United Distillers to the nation as a 'living museum' of distilling. A delightful magnet for tourists, it lies complete and perfectly preserved. Though its single malt can still be bought, Dallas Dhu no longer distils. However, it cannot be termed a lost distillery.

Pittyvaich-Glenlivet was opened at Dufftown in 1973 by Arthur Bell and Sons as a sister distillery to Dufftown-Glenlivet. It continued to distil under the UD banner but was mothballed in 1993, with scant likelihood of reinstatement. However, it is being used as a research and equipment-testing centre and is still very much a complete operation. For that reason, a 'lost' label seems at present inappropriate.

Three definite recent losses to add to the existing list are Coleburn, near Elgin, Convalmore at Dufftown and Glengarioch at Oldmeldrum. Even as I write, more distilleries in the area are joining the 'mothballed' list but for most if not all of them, such mothballing should be temporary.

Banff, Inverboyndie, Banffshire (1863-1983)

Benachie (*aka* Jericho), near Insch, Aberdeenshire (1822-1915)

Coleburn, near Elgin (1897-1985)

Convalmore, Dufftown (1894-1985)

Glenaden, Old Deer, Aberdeenshire (1882-1915)

Glengarioch, Oldmeldrum, Aberdeenshire (1798-1995)

Glenugie, (*aka* Invernettie), near Peterhead, Aberdeenshire (1821-1983)

Glen Cawdor, Nairn (1898-1927)

Parkmore, Dufftown (1894-1931)

Speyside, Kingussie (1895-1911)

Towiemore, Botriphnie, Banffshire (1896-1930)

BANFF, *Inverboyndie*

Whatever else one can say about Banff distillery, one cannot complain about it having a dull history. It is a fascinating narrative which, for once, is singularly well documented. It has witnessed fires, explosions, bombings and other events. It is truly sad the distillery is no longer there: tourist guides might have kept visitors enthralled all day long with their tales of bygone dramas.

The original distillery was founded at Mill of Banff near Colleonard Farm in 1824 by Major James McKilligan, who operated it for 13 years until his death. It was taken over by Alex Mackay and later, in 1852, by James Simpson and his son, James junior. A decade on, this partnership was dissolved and in 1863 the son built a new distillery at Inverboyndie, one mile south-west of Banff beside the railway line that had been opened in 1859. The site was chosen both for rail proximity (private sidings were built soon afterwards) and a better water supply.

The first of the dramas came on 9 May 1877, when the main distillery was completely destroyed by fire, although maltings and warehouses were untouched. Rapid rebuilding saw it back in action in October, with the distillery's own private fire engine kept permanently on site thereafter.

The distillery grew and prospered, with six operating stills and an annual output of 200,000 gallons by the mid-1880s. It became a limited company in November 1898 with an estimated capital value of £72,000. All the directors and the manager were Simpsons. In 1921 they sold a big slice of the equity to London-based Mile End Distillery Company, a subsidiary of the brewers Taylor Walker. One of the Banff warehouses became a blending, filling and bottling store, making the establishment a major local employer. But the grim 1920s and the slump took their toll; Simpson and Co went into voluntary liquidation in March 1932 and the distillery was bought by SMD for £50,000. It stayed closed for several years and again was shut for the duration of the war, during which soldiers were billeted in the barley lofts and Nissen huts built on site.

The day Banff will never forget was 16 August 1941, when a solitary German Junkers Ju-88 bomber strafed the malt barns with gunfire and bombed No 12 warehouse, setting its hundreds of casks of spirit on fire. Exploding butts of whisky spun through the air and rivers of blue fire flowed from the building.

Casks were hurriedly smashed to stop the fire spreading and thousands of gallons gurgled into watercourses and oozed onto adjacent farmland. Ducks, geese and other waterfowl were found flapping drunkenly on the beach beside the Boyndie Burn outflow and cows missed a day's milking because they could not get on their feet.

Amid all the chaos, the strong hand of authority prevailed. One astute fireman, who used his helmet to rescue spirit flowing to waste and shared this unorthodox brimming goblet with colleagues, wound up in court! That night Lord Haw-Haw claimed on the news bulletin from Berlin that the Luftwaffe had destroyed 'a major ammunition depot' in northern Scotland. The truth, if anything, was far sadder...

Production restarted after the war and continued with little let-up bar the odd silent season. As with most malt distilleries in that era, all output went for blending. An unexpected drama was to unfold on 3 October 1959, when a coppersmith who was brazing on a new section of copper pipe to the spirit still, caused a violent explosion. The spirit still and a large part of the distillery were wrecked and took weeks to repair. Miraculously, neither the coppersmith, Norman Forbes from Dufftown, nor the man assisting him, Banff man Alex Kemp, were injured though both were badly shaken. The fact the distillery was closed while the still repair was being done undoubtedly minimised the damage. The sequel came in January 1960, when Scottish Malt Distillers were found guilty at Banff Sheriff Court of contravening safety regulations and were fined £15...

Output from Banff soon resumed and continued for another third of a century. Then, however, it was among a clutch of distilleries earmarked for closure in 1983. It closed on 31 May, putting 14 people out of work. Demolition of all distillery buildings and warehouses bar one started in 1985. The last one was being demolished when it was destroyed by a bad fire on 11 April 1991, obliterating the final trace of what had been the Banff area's largest industrial site for well over a century.

An interesting footnote is that in the mid-1960s SMD had applied for, and obtained, planning permission for a replacement distillery at Inverboyndie industrial estate, but the plans were never activated. A business consortium put forward plans some years later for a distillery near Duff House. Again permission was granted, but again nothing was done. Distilling has now ceased at Banff, though there is a distillery at Macduff and Glenglassaugh Distillery, a few miles west of Banff, was restored after 60 years of almost constant disuse but is now again mothballed.

BENACHIE, *near Insch*

The relationship between Kirk and distilling in Scotland has long been a fraught one, the church being associated with temperance and abstinence. With that in mind, a distillery called Jericho which took its water from a stream called the Jordan might be looked on as trying to be too holy for its own good. Yet such a distillery did exist and, although distilling ceased nearly 80 years ago, the ruined buildings still stand and the Jordan still flows.

The distillery was started at Nether Jericho farm, in the shadow of Bennachie, between 1822 and 1824 by William Smith and the spirit was advertised in Aberdeen newspapers by late 1824. The distillery prospered under Mr Smith for some 40 years. In 1864, the tenancy of farm and distillery passed to John Maitland who ran it for two decades. He died in the early 1880s and both tenancies were acquired by brothers-in-law William Callander and John Graham. They renamed the distillery Benachie (with one 'N'), drew up and implimented plans to extend and improve it – and even devised an advertising slogan *There's nae sair heids in Benachie*, that may have generally indicated that the whisky was a light malt or simply that they were marketing men without knowing it!

Benachie Distillery, c1910

The next 30 years appear to have been the zenith of the establishment. Output rose from 25,000 gallons a year in the mid-1880s to nearer 50,000 and carts pulled by hefty Clydesdales trundled daily to Insch station, each bearing three casks of malt bound for distant customers. Regular convoys of farmcarts delivered barley to Jericho, the carters frequently heading home far from sober thanks to the generous drams offered to them at the distillery. However, those were easier-going times and the horses doubtless knew the way home anyway. In addition to the distillery's licensed house and grocery outlets, the whisky was sold in two-gallon ceramic 'pigs' and bottles from the company's own shop at Insch. As late as 1906, two gallons of cask-strength whisky from the distillery cost a princely 35 shillings – which barely pays for a single dram in some establishments today. There are at least two ceramic Benachie pigs in existence – both empty – and various memorabilia are known to be scattered across Scotland.

However, the cumulative effects of the 1909 excise duty rises and other factors affected Benachie's fortunes and it ceased distilling in 1913, though whisky was still available from local pubs and outlets until well into World War I. Members of the family and business colleagues floated a scheme to restart the distillery in 1920 and provisionally registered a company with a capital of £2,000. However, their plans never came to fruition and the company was finally wound up in 1960.

The farm still exists though the buildings housing the distillery have largely fallen down or been demolished. However, bars on many windows tell the informed visitor that this was once indeed a distillery. Very old folk in the Garioch still tell of dances and hoolies in the disused malt barns 70 or so years ago. In mid-1993, an Inverurie businessman launched a vatted malt under the name Bennachie which has since enjoyed considerable success. All is not lost...

COLEBURN, *near Elgin*

A small distillery lost in a cluster of them south of Elgin, Coleburn was built in 1897 by the Dundee blenders John Robertson. Among its illustrious neighbours is Linkwood Distillery. Information on the distillery is scant, but it is thought to have had two stills originally and drew its process water from a nearby spring in the Glen of Rothes.

Coleburn Distillery, near Elgin, 1997. The kiln is on the left with the stillhouse to the right

Robertsons sold the distillery in 1916 to Clynelish, at that time a consortium of DCL, John Risk and John Walker, who eventually passed it to SMD in 1930. It continued to operate quietly for more than 60 years under the DCL/SMD banner, though licensed to their subsidiary J & G Stewart of Edinburgh, and passed with the DCL portfolio to UD after the Guinness takeover. As with many less well-known distilleries, virtually all output went to the blenders.

Being a small distillery with largely outmoded plant, it was a prime candidate for mothballing and in 1985 SMD did so during the mid-80s downturn. It stood idle for nearly a decade, then in the mid-1990s United Distillers sought planning permission to convert the distillery buildings into residential flats and houses. After much discussion, the local authority agreed by one vote to the plan in March 1996 but objections from various sources have persisted and conversion work has yet to start.

It is a distillery that is still relatively intact, and it is understood almost all the production plant is still in situ. Its single malt can still be obtained from specialist bottlers.

CONVALMORE, *Dufftown*

This is a distillery with quite an interesting history. It is still standing and is currently owned by William Grant & Sons, of Glenfiddich, Balvenie and Standfast fame, though they have no plans whatsoever to put it back into use.

It was built near Dufftown in 1894 by the Convalmore-Glenlivet Distillery Co Ltd and drew its process water from springs in the Conval Hills. Like many distilleries built in that late-Victorian boom, it saw its operators fall on hard times as the Edwardian recession bit and in 1904 the distillery was sold to W&P Lowrie, who in turn were taken over two years later by the London-based James Buchanan & Co.

Buchanan's were one of the few firms to thrive during the Edwardian era and they rebuilt the distillery in 1909-10, installing an experimental continuous distillation system to make malt spirit. There are no records or indications of whether the system was a success or not.

Convalmore was among several Buchanan distilleries taken over by DCL in 1925 and passed to SMD in 1930. Since then it has known the odd silent season, was mothballed during the war and then expanded in 1964 in the great post-war Scotch boom. Capacity was enlarged from two stills to four, warehousing increased and a dark grains plant built alongside to process draff and pot ale from both Convalmore and other SMD distilleries in the area.

Convalmore Distillery, Dufftown, 1997

Convalmore was mothballed in 1985 by SMD and was sold with the dark grains plant to William Grant & Sons a few years later. Grants demolished the dark grains plant in 1995 and use Convalmore's many warehouses to store casks of Glenfiddich and Balvenie. All distilling plant and other equipment has been stripped out of Convalmore, although externally it looks largely complete.

Wm Grant have no plans to reinstate Convalmore, though it will probably stand for many years yet. Its pleasant single malt is widely available from specialist bottlers, a distictive memory of a distinctive lost distillery.

GLENADEN, *Old Deer*

One of the smallest in Scotland, Glenaden was a farm-based distillery established in 1845 by Messrs Milne and Co who already ran a brewery at nearby Biffie Farm. It was sold to new operators, George J. Wilson & Co in 1882 and they in turn sold it to T. Yelton Ogilvie & Co about the turn of the century. Wilsons also took on the operation of Biffie brewery but it is not recorded whether this passed to Yelton Ogilvie.

As with many small or marginal distilleries in the early 1900s, the effects of increased excise duty and failing demand took their toll. Things went further downhill in the years prior to World War I and the distillery was closed by 1915. Very little information is available, other than that Glenaden used locally sourced barley and took its water from Biffie springs. At its peak, output was about 12,000 gallons a year.

GLENGARIOCH, *Oldmeldrum*

This is a notable distillery with a long history – it just failed to celebrate its bicentenary – and several claims to fame. It first started distilling in the late-18th century under Thomas Simpson, then was closed for several years before being revived by Ingram, Lamb and Co who ran it from 1827-33. Then in 1837 it was acquired by John Manson, who ran the nearby Strathmeldrum distillery and who eventually sold that to concentrate on Glengarioch – pronounced 'glen geerie' – and run it until 1884.

At that point the distillery was bought, either from Manson or his family, by J F Thomson & Co of Leith. Barnard visited two years later and described two barley lofts, two malting floors, a peat-fired kiln, a neat little mill with a pair of malt rollers, a mashing machine feeding a shallow 14ft mash tun that fed wort to five washbacks holding 3,000 gallons each. At the time the distillery had two almost-new stills of 1,900 and 1,500 gallons respectively with worms cooled in a vast 40ft worm tub. Casks were kept in three large bonded warehouses and annual output was a modest 50,000 gallons.

Around 1909-10 the distillery passed from the Thomsons to the Glengarioch Distillery Co Ltd, whose MD was the famous William Sanderson of Leith. Sanderson's operated it until 1940 when they sold it to Booth's Distilleries – of gin fame – who kept it silent for three years and sold it on in 1943 to SMD.

After the war SMD reactivated the plant and ran Glengarioch until 1968 when ongoing problems with the sourcing of process water led them to close it down. It was bought in 1970 by Stanley P Morrison, a small independent distilling group who also own Bowmore and Auchentoshan and who are now wholly owned by Suntory of Japan. They drilled deeper for water, put in a third still and switched from coal fuel to oil, demolishing the old chimney in 1975. They also installed a visitor centre at a time when they were unheard of. Furthermore, they showed great initiative in 1976 by building numerous hothouses in which they grew several hundred

Glengarioch Distillery, Oldmeldrum, 1997

tonnes of tomatoes a year by utilising the waste heat from the distilling process. At one point, the tomato side of the business employed almost as many people as the whisky side. However, cheap tomatoes from the continent eventually undermined the scheme's success and it was phased out in the early 1990s.

As a single malt, Glengarioch never reached the heights of approval won by Bowmore and the new owners Suntory eventually decided to close the distillery. Plans were submitted in 1995 to convert it into 14 dwellings and build 86 houses on the remainder of the site. There were numerous local objections, the plans were never fully approved and (at the time of writing) the matter is still in limbo.

In the summer of 1995 the distillery was finally closed, with the loss of six jobs, well down from the 17 or 18 it had employed several years before. In late 1995 the Bennachie Whisky Co of Inverurie made an offer to buy the distillery, but those plans apparently ran into the sand.

At present the distillery stands silent and unused, with no sign of the housing proposals receiving approval from the local authority. At another time, one could have hoped that some white knight of the whisky world would come galloping up, cheque book in hand, ready to buy up and restore this little gem. But in the late 1990s, it is utterly unlikely. Sadly, Glengarioch must now rate as a lost distillery. However, its nectar is still widely sold in various ages and strengths and is well worth buying as one of the most inexpensive and underrated single malts.

GLENUGIE, *near Peterhead*

Few distilleries have had such a long and complicated history as Glenugie. It is built on the site of an old windmill, remnants of which still survive, and is overlooked by a ruined watchtower on a small eminence. Originally called Invernettie – after the area where it stands – it started up in 1833-34 under the banner of Donald, McLeod & Co. In 1837 it was renamed Glenugie Distillery Co and converted to a brewery. Then in 1875 it was rebuilt on a far larger scale as a distillery by Scottish Highland Distillers Co Ltd, with an annual output of 90,000 gallons. Alas, within a few years the firm was moribund and was wound up in 1879.

The remains of Glenugie Distillery in 1993

The distillery was sold to George Whyte & Co, which had no more luck and was sequestered in 1882. It was bought in 1884 by Simon Forbes, who seems to be the first person to exploit Glenugie successfully, running the business until 1915 or later. It closed for much of World War I, operated briefly as Glenugie Distillery Ltd 1923-24, then was silent from 1925-37.

In that year the name Glenugie Distillery Ltd was revived as a new company, owned by a London firm, Seager Evans and Co Ltd, which had acquired several other Scots distilleries both before and after the war. In 1956, Seager Evans was taken over by US-based Schenley Industries Inc, which eventually put all its Scottish distilleries under the umbrella of Long John Distillers Ltd.

Prior to the Schenley takeover, Glenugie was briefly acquired by Hugh Fraser (later Lord Fraser of Allander), but the company was wound up in 1958 and its assets transferred to Long John. The Seager Evans company was reconstituted as Long John International in 1975 and sold to the British brewing group Whitbread.

Schenley, on acquiring Glenugie in 1956, invested heavily in the distillery. It was completely refurbished, with new plant and equipment installed including an oil-fired boiler to replace the coal-fired system. Process water was piped in from several miles away. Two new stills were installed and fitted with big condensers rather than the old-fashioned worm coils. The wash still had a 200-tube condenser, the spirit still a 50-tube one. Production was doubled, and this immediately strained the warehousing to capacity. That problem was solved in 1963 when on-site malting was discontinued and the maltings converted to bonded storage. Eventually the site had nine bonded warehouses with a total capacity of 1.5 million gallons. Over a century and a half, the site had grown from four to 25 acres.

Glenugie was among the many distilleries mothballed in the early-1980s downturn and was closed by Whitbread in 1983. Had it been in any other part of Scotland, it might have been kept with an eye to being reopened in the future. But Peterhead was in the ferment of North Sea oil and industrial premises were in high demand. Not long after its closure, the premises were split and acquired by two North Sea oil engineering firms. Glenugie is unlikely ever to work as a distillery again.

GLEN CAWDOR, *Nairn*

Glen Cawdor was one of 16 distilleries built in the late Victorian boom prior to the early Edwardian bust. Its lifespan was barely 30 years and, although it built up a good reputation in its day, information about it is relatively scant.

It was built near the River Nairn close to the railway viaduct bearing the Inverness-Elgin line across the river. The location was close to a hollow alive with many small, clear springs which bubbled to the sandy surface, doubtless prompting the idea it would be a good distillery site. In 1896 three businessmen, Messrs D. McAndie of Inverness, James Mill of Nairn and James Mackillican of Calcutta, bought six acres of land and established the Glencawdor Distillery Company.

Building began in July 1896, based on plans from Charles Doig, the noted distillery architect from Elgin who created the famous malt-kiln 'pagoda roof' and designed efficient, cost-effective plants. Distilling started in October 1897. Working barley capacity was 800 bushels, mainly locally-sourced. Peats came from the Kildrummie Moss south-west of Nairn, mashing and cooling water came from the springs. The pot ale and spent lees went into a storage tank for

Distillery workers at Glen Cawdor, c1905

collection by farmers. Unused effluent was piped to Nairn town's new sewage farm. It was a model establishment by late Victorian standards and its 100ft main chimney became an instant and definitive landmark.

Alas, it opened on the crest of the wave and fell into the early 20th century trough. The company was dissolved in 1901 and the distillery acquired in 1903 by John Haig and Co, of Markinch, Fife. They operated it for 24 years until the late-1920s slump obliged them to undertake a general retrenchment. The distillery was closed in 1927 and demolished around 1930, the stone being used to help build Broadhill housing estate. Of the distillery, nothing remains today and the site is now playing fields. In terms of both archeological and archival remains, Glen Cawdor has disappeared almost without trace.

PARKMORE, *Dufftown*

Parkmore dates from the same period as Glen Cawdor, being built at Dufftown in the great 1890s whisky boom by the Parkmore Distillery Company Ltd. The main difference with Glen Cawdor is that it is still almost perfectly preserved today, though distillation has not taken place there for nigh on 60 years.

A substantial distillery with a classic pagoda roof and acres of

Parkmore Distillery. . . perfectly preserved, 1993

warehouses, Parkmore too fell quickly on hard times, was taken over by Dundee-based James Watson and Co in 1900, which in turn was acquired by John Dewar and Sons Ltd in 1923. The distillery was passed to DCL in 1925 and from them to SMD in 1930. It was reported as being silent from 1931, though it was still licensed to Daniel Crawford and Son Ltd as late as 1940.

Its location in Dufftown and massive warehousing capacity has probably been its salvation. Had it been elsewhere and with scant storage, it might well have been bulldozed years ago. It is used for warehousing and bonded storage to this day and is described as 'externally the most perfect survivor of the late-1890s boom in distilleries'. Of its whisky and folklore I could find nothing.

SPEYSIDE, *Kingussie*

Speyside is one of those very rare distilleries where the magic runes of whisky-making somehow did not work out. It was a fine distillery in the right area, with good financial backing and one of the era's best managers. Its water source was said to be excellent, the distillery plant, equipment, casks and raw materials were as good as, or superior to, those of other Speyside distilleries. Yet for some reason or another, things did not work out for this most southerly of the Spey producers.

The distillery was the work of two men, both called George Grant. One became distillery manager at Glen Grant in 1875, aged just 24, and his vision and skills are credited with making Glen Grant one of the great names of whisky. However, he had to retire due to ill-health in 1893 – just when the Laird of Ballindalloch, Sir George MacPherson Grant, was nurturing the idea of a distillery at Kingussie to share in the whisky boom further down the Spey. Sir George persuaded Mr George to take up the challenge.

The Speyside Distillery Co Ltd was floated, the plans drawn up by a local architect, work soon started and the £20,000 distillery came on-stream in 1895. It was a handsome complex built of locally-sourced stone forming three sides of a square west of the village and overlooked by Ruthven Barracks. It stood on 10 acres behind the Gordon Arms Hotel and beside the Gynack (or Guynach) Burn, which provided process and power water, with a good approach road and private siding from the Perth-Inverness rail line. Rail wagons moved directly under a hoist that lifted the barley sacks to the vast loft and draff was direct-loaded into the trucks as well.

Under the loft were two steeps and two large malting floors, supported by blue-painted cast-iron columns. The kilns had perforated iron floor plates and, unusually, revolving extractor cowls. The malt mill was powered by a 16hp steam engine or an 18ft 6in water wheel turned by the Gynack mill lade. Worts from the mash-tun were cooled by a Morton's vertical refrigerator and fermented in one of six 9,000-gallon washbacks. A 7,200 gallon wash-charger filled the 3,500 gallon wash still, which in turn supplied the 2,700 gallon spirit still. Both of these had reflux bulges at the base of their necks. Casks were filled from a wooden 3,700 gallon spirit vat and stored in three large warehouses.

Speyside also had electricity and phone links with the railway station and Old Milton, the residence of the managing director, John MacPherson Grant, the laird's son. Shortly after the distillery opened, George Grant left and in late 1897 bought a licensed grocer's shop in Lossiemouth. He was there only eight months when he died in July 1898, aged 47. His successor at the distillery was James Cumming, from Rothes.

Just what didn't quite work at Speyside is unrecorded, but from the start there were worries and problems. The great Charles C. Doig was called in to advise on what might be wrong. There is no record of his diagnosis, nor whether remedial action, if any, was taken. The distillery struggled on into the 20th century but distilling seems to have stopped between 1905-10. The buildings were sold for just £750 and were then largely demolished. One house was spared, as was one other edifice which became a masonic lodge and a printing works. The company was wound up in 1911.

It is thought some of the plant and equipment was bought and installed at other distilleries; Speyside's worm tub went to Dalwhinnie, survived that distillery's catastrophic fire of 1934 and was finally replaced by condensers in 1986. After the 1934 fire, Dalwhinnie acquired some other second-hand equipment, much of it from another ill-fated North-east distillery, Towiemore.

Yet Speyside's story actually ends on a bright note. A new distillery bearing the same name opened not far away in 1990. Built beside the River Tromie, the new Speyside was a near-lifelong dream for George Christie, one of the industry's great independents, who launched Strathmore/North of Scotland grain distillery at Cambus, Clackmannanshire, in the late 1950s.

Work on Speyside started back in the 1960s, but the distillery only opened in 1990, one of a tiny handful of new distilleries to open in Scotland in recent times. A young malt from the distillery, Drumguish, is already on the market but a 10-year-old Speyside will only be with us in the new millennium. From the whispers in the industry, it will be well worth waiting for.

A final interesting note is that George Christie bought and retired to Old Milton, where the MacPherson Grants kept in touch by phone with the original Speyside Distillery. Parts of that phone system are said still to be sunk in the ground and the walls. . .

TOWIEMORE, *Botriphnie, Banffshire*

We tend to take for granted the platitude that Scotland's soft water, clear air and tangy peat, plus the peerless skills of its distillers and maltsters, make its malt whiskies such world-beaters. But every now and again one comes across a distillery where these ingredients turned out to be less than infallible. Parkmore and Speyside distilleries are said to have had such problems. Towiemore is another example.

Towiemore, say the dwindling few who have drunk it and whose tastebuds have long memories, was an excellent whisky. But it had a problem: when water was added to it often went cloudy, like Pernod or Ouzo. Though the haziness dispersed quickly, it was enough to disconcert some drinkers and around 1922 the blenders told the distillery they would no longer accept Towiemore for blending. It was a fatal blow. The problem was said to be intermittent, possibly caused by lime in the water. Filtration and other water treatment was tried but not with complete success. The quirk may not have been the only nail in Towiemore's coffin, but it was certainly the deciding one.

Towiemore was floated by Mr Peter Dawson in July 1897, and construction started in November on a large site beside the Keith-Dufftown rail line. In 1898, the just-complete distillery was acquired by the Towiemore-Glenlivet Distillery Co Ltd. There was a dispute over shares in early 1902 although that did not delay building a new warehouse later that year. There was a fire at the distillery in November 1904, but for the most part those times were uneventful.

It closed during World War I, the axe falling in July 1917. The company restarted after the war, but went into liquidation in 1930. SMD then bought the distillery and closed it. However, the maltings and warehouses were kept in use until recently and a portion of the maltings were converted into agricultural engineering premises in 1993.

The East Coast And Tayside

Although the East coast of Scotland lacks the grandeur and glamour of the Highlands and the West coast, it has much to commend it. Three of Scotland's four main cities lie on it and fertile farming areas abound along it where generations ago new plots and farmsteads were established to grow the hardy northern barley variant, bigg – hence the plethora of villages and hamlets called Newbigging.

It was also an area of many distilleries, though some had a precarious existence. Scores of tiny distilleries flowered briefly in Perthshire in the heady days of the early 1800s. Over the past century about a dozen notable distilleries grew, expanded and expired in what is now Tayside and eastern Grampian. Several have closed since 1980 and, as with certain Speyside distilleries, it is sometimes difficult to draw a definite line between those which are closed for good and those which are just mothballed.

However, in the last decade of the 20th century several distilleries have sadly moved from the 'mothballed' into the 'lost' category. Among these are Stonehaven's Glenury Royal, which was closed in February 1982 by SMD less than 20 years after a mid-1960s expansion and refurbishment. Although hopes of its reopening were always slender, the point of no return was passed in September 1993 when planning permission for housing on the site was granted. A similar 'pending' label long hung over Montrose's Lochside Distillery, but it too seems about to go, as has its near neighbour, Glenesk.

Sadly, Brechin's North Port Distillery has vanished. It was closed in 1983 and its vital main chimney demolished a few years later. Although it stood for more than a decade, it was demolished in the mid-1990s to make way for a supermarket. Happily, the future of

Brechin's other distillery, Glencadam, seems reasonably secure as part of the Allied Distillers group.

Therefore, the list of East Coast lost distilleries reads as follows:

Auchnagie (*aka* Easter Tullymet, Achnagie), Tulliemet, near Ballinluig, Perthshire (1827-1912)

Auchinblae, Kincardineshire (1896-1926)

Ballechin, near Ballinluig (1810-1927)

Bon Accord (*aka* North of Scotland), Aberdeen (1855-1910)

Devanha, Aberdeen (1827-1915)

Glencoull, Justinhaugh, Angus (1897-1929)

Glenesk, Montrose (1897-1983)

Glenury Royal, Stonehaven (1826-1986)

Grandtully, near Aberfeldy, Perthshire (1825-1910)

Isla (*aka* Clockserrie), Bridgend, Perth (1851-1926)

Lochside, Montrose (1957-92)

North Port (*aka* Townhead, or Brechin), Brechin (1820-1983)

Strathdee, Aberdeen (1821-c1945)

Stronachie, Forgandenny, Perthshire (1900-28)

AUCHNAGIE

Tulliemet, near Ballinluig, Perthshire

The Ballinluig area once had several small distilleries, all since long gone. They were farm-based distilleries that aimed to 'add value' to local barley and provide spirits to local merchants and hostelries which were largely isolated from other suppliers until the coming of the railways. Three were to survive until this century – Grandtully, Ballechin and Auchnagie. Also, two of the smallest operations surviving today, Edradour and Glenturret, belong in the category of originally farm-based Perthshire distilleries.

Auchnagie, first built in about 1812, had a varied and precarious existence. Records show it under a cavalcade of owners down the years – James Duff (1827-33), Duncan Scott (1860-62), Forbes & Co (1867-78), Alex McLaughlan (1882), John McLaren (1882-84) and Peter Dawson (1887-88). It was finally acquired in 1890 by the

Auchnagie Distillery buildings, 1993

mighty Perth-based John Dewar and Sons Ltd, who ran it until 1912 when they closed it down and subsequently dismantled it.

During Peter Dawson's short tenure it was visited by Alfred Barnard whose description is singularly brief since it was a warm summer and the distillery was closed – the temperatures being too high for malting. His minimal portrait nonetheless mentions an annual output of 19,000 to 24,000 gallons and warehouse space for 40,000 gallons. Water was sourced from the Auchnagie Hills, the barley from local farmers and the peat from Loch Broom. His final paragraph is a classic.

> *One exciseman is employed at the distillery, who informed us he leads quite a pastoral life here and spends his summer days in his garden and little farmyard.*

Of the distillery little remains, although the spirit store and some walls still stand, a quiet rural monument to Auchnagie's century of distilling.

AUCHINBLAE, *Kincardineshire*

Auchinblae was built in the late boom of the 1890s and, despite initial success, had neither the depth of expertise nor the financial muscle to survive the grim plague that decimated the industry in the 1920s.

The present owner has kept the original water supply rights and maintained the vast cistern that stored the distillery's process water.

The distillery buildings were originally a spinning mill built in 1795 bestriding the Luther Water (rhymes with 'mother' with a soft 'th') which flows in a deepish cleft south-west of the village. The mill, which had its own gasworks which also supplied the village, closed in the early 1890s. The possibility of converting it to a distillery was mooted and, after two experts praised the excellence of the local water, the Auchinblae Distillery Company Ltd was floated in 1895 with a capital of £20,000 (later raised to £25,000) in £1 shares, a large number of which were taken up more than 200 people in and around the village.

Auchinblae Distillery's kiln, still standing in 1993

It was no small venture. The distillery design was entrusted to the great Charles C. Doig and his plans to convert the mill turned into a massive task. The Luther Water was dammed and a US-built water-driven turbine and generator were imported and installed to provide electricity for the works and manager's house. To get the best process water in the area, a three inch pipe was run nearly a mile from an uphill spring at Templebank to a large cistern above the distillery, enclosed in a stone-built, slate-roofed building that stands to this day. Last but not least, a sturdy iron bridge was built across the Luther Water to enable horse-drawn carts easy access to the distillery, which in its mill days could only be reached by a steep incline.

Commendably for its time, the distillery owners rated safety highly and had three fire hydrants and hoses installed at strategic locations on the premises. Like all Doig distilleries, it had a pagoda roof to the malt kiln and was highly efficient and economical by the norms of its era. There were conveyor systems for barley and malt, a draff screw to empty the mash tun, four 6,000-gallon washbacks, a 1,500-gallon wash still and slightly smaller spirit still. The spirit store measured 90ft square. The first manager was recruited from Ord distillery at Muir of Ord and production is thought to have started in late 1896.

Relatively little is known of the distillery's 20-plus years in operation. Its whisky was certainly drinkable if not notable and it was a valuable outlet for local barley and peat, as well as a source of draff, employment and investment for many local people.

Auchinblae went into liquidation in 1916. It was acquired by Macdonald Greenlees, Williams (Distillers) Ltd – who took over Stronachie at Forgandenny about the same time. MGW were eventually absorbed by SMD. Distilling stopped in July 1929 and Auchinblae finally closed in 1930. James Steven, Stronachie's former manager, saw to the disposal of the spirits in the bonded warehouse before he retired to Burrelton in Perthshire.

Demolition soon started on the production buildings. In 1933 the whole site was bought by John Thomson, a motor mechanic, who turned the remaining buildings (mainly warehouses on the Luther's eastern bank) into a garage. He had the great chimney demolished and the top ring of coping stones forms the centrepiece of the garden today. In 1954 Mr Thomson acquired the other garage in Auchinblae and decided to move the business there, though the family stayed on in the big house. Until that year the house was lit by electricity from the turbine – and switching off the lights last thing at night meant walking up to the sluice and blocking off the mill lade. In 1954, the sluice and mill lade were taken down and the house connected to the local hydro-electric supply. But the turbine is still there today, a unique item of local industrial history. John Thomson's family still live in the house and his daughter, Ann Thomson, possesses the only known bottle, alas empty, of Auchinblae Highland Whisky.

BALLECHIN, *near Ballinluig, Perthshire*

Ballechin has much in common with its close neighbour, Auchnagie. It was built about the same time (1810), also by a group of farmers. It also had its own special water source (a deep spring only yards from the distillery), many owners or operators over the decades, a modest output (18,000 gallons a year) and was finally eclipsed in the industry's nadir years earlier this century. It was, however, to outlast Auchnagie by 20 years: it was silent from 1927, but the stored whisky was not finally disposed of until late 1933.

The list of operators includes Peter Kennedy (1818-19), James Robertson (1821-30), George Robinson (1833), then Robert Kennedy for 40 years from 1835-75 and beyond. All of them were related or connected to the distillery's founders. In 1875 the distillery was acquired by Robertson and Sons, said to be first outsiders. However, they were the most successful operators, keeping Ballechin going until the years prior to World War I. The distillery opened again in 1923 under William Rose, who had bought the entire estate, but it closed finally around 1927.

Mr Rose died in the early 1930s and his estate was bought by one R. Wemyss Honeyman who made clear he had no intentions of restarting the distillery and ordered all the stored whisky to be sold. The sale took place in late 1932 and the last casks were removed from the bonded warehouses in early December 1933. 'A propitious

The remains of Ballechin Distillery, 1993

time', noted an article in the *Perthshire Advertiser*; with US prohibition now a thing of the past, there was a renewed market for good malt whisky.

Some buildings are still used by the farm and many amateur historians make pilgrimages to see the outer shell of Ballechin, now devoid of its copper soul.

BON ACCORD, *Hardgate, Aberdeen*

In the 1820s Aberdeen saw a spate of small distilleries established, most of which stumbled into oblivion within a couple of decades. Slightly more durable was the Union Glen distillery which ended up in sequestration in 1853. A year later an adjacent brewery dating from 1785 went bust and an astute business group decided to combine the two, transferring Union Glen's distilling equipment into the bankrupt brewery and opening it as the Bon-Accord Distillery in 1855, which was formally changed to a limited company in 1876.

It was to prove very successful, becoming the largest pot-still distillery in the North of Scotland with an annual output of some 300,000 gallons. The owners also showed an early global vision, concentrating all output on export and on-ship sales, with no whisky going to the home market or to the blenders. It had its own bottling and casing plant, with thousands of bottles of Cock O' The North shuttling from bond to docks every week.

Not that everything went without a hitch. The distillery suffered three fires over the years, the worst – in 1885 – halting production for several months. Indeed, it seems it never fully recovered from that blaze and the Bon Accord Distillery Co Ltd was wound up in 1896. It was taken over by Dailuaine-Talisker Distilleries Ltd, who renamed it the North of Scotland Distillery. However, it failed to thrive under its new ownership, drifted downhill and closed shortly before World War I. No known vestiges of the buildings remain and part of the site is now housing. The Ferry Burn which flowed openly past it in Barnard's day is long since culverted and out of sight – though it still runs its stygian way down to the River Dee.

DEVANHA, *Aberdeen*

Devanha Brewery (named after the area of Aberdeen in which it stood) was established in the early 1820s, on a site north-west of the Dee on its last major bend before the sea – a site subsequently sandwiched between river and railway when the latter was built 30 years later. Devanha's owners decided to add a distillery in 1837 and established the Devanha Distillery Company. The distilling side was acquired in 1852 by William Black and Co, who operated the distillery until 1910.

The site was further constricted when the city of Aberdeen opted to build a fine esplanade, now called Riverside Drive, upriver from the harbour area for the then princely sum of £95,000. However, it certainly improved road access to the distillery.

The only available description of Devanha comes from Alfred Barnard, who portrayed the establishment as granite-built, substantial and well-equipped, with four bonded warehouses, a 25hp steam engine, two large stills in the main building and two small ancient stills dating from the distillery's infancy in another building. Process water came, unromantically, from the town's mains supply, though cooling and condensing water came from the Dee. Annual output was a substantial 220,000 gallons and the modern bonds could hold 6,000 hogsheads.

Not unlike its rival Bon Accord, Devanha went into decline in the Edwardian era and, although it was possibly acquired by new owners around 1910, it had irrevocably shut its doors by 1915. The buildings, though much modified, are largely still standing and the words 'Devanha Distillery' are still visible on the roof slates and can be seen by passing rail travellers.

GLEN COULL, *Justinhaugh, near Forfar*

Thirty or so miles south-west of Auchinblae lies what was once Glen Coull distillery, the lifespan of which bears quite a resemblance to that of Auchinblae. The one difference is that Glen Coull started as a grain mill, was converted to a distillery in 1897 and was then converted back to a grain mill around 1930. The distillery stood beside the River South Esk at Justinhaugh, a locality near Tannadice close to Oathlaw station on the then Forfar-Brechin branch line.

The distillery was first operated as a partnership between George Willsher, a Dundee wine and spirit merchant, and George Duncan, a distiller originally from Limavady in what is now Northern Ireland. The distillery manager was Mr J.A. Gordon, who remained as such throughout Glen Coull's three decades. Mr Willsher had originally hoped to buy the Cameron Bridge distillery at Markinch but had been unable to obtain the transfer of the necessary water rights. They therefore opted for Glen Coull. Their partnership, however, quickly hit problems and was dissolved in 1899, with George Duncan departing. A feu charter for the distillery and surrounding land was granted by the estate owner, Major John Wedderburn Ogilvy of Ruthven, to George Willsher and Son in May 1901. The document referred to Glen Coull Mill – though this, it seems, was not unusual. A mill had acceptable rural connotations whereas a distillery was linked to 'trade' and hard drinking, so a degree of descriptive discretion was not unheard of.

George Willsher ran Glen Coull for more than a decade, becoming a limited company in 1908, which was eventually bankrupted in 1912-13. Dundee accountant William Pattullo was appointed liquidator and the distillery was among assets sold in May 1913 to George Duncan, who in the meantime had become distiller at Dean Distillery, Edinburgh. He ran Glen Coull until 1927 when, faced with the unremitting gloom of the times, he closed it down. However, distillery closures, especially in a recession, are a long process. After distilling stops, there are thousands of gallons of young spirit standing in bonded warehouses – a valuable asset but one that takes time to dispose of.

The distillery was converted to a mill sometime in the early 1930s, with the high stack being demolished on 29 July 1934, and its bricks being used to convert the bonded warehouses into modern piggeries by the new owners, J.A. Whamond (or Whammond) & Son Ltd. They changed the company name to The Angus Milling Company Ltd in 1936. AMC was acquired by Hamlyn Milling after the war and Hamlyn was taken over by the J. Bibby group in 1992. Bibby's transferred production elsewhere and demolished most of the production buildings.

Glen Coull mill today is very different to its distillery days but the mill lade (which used water both from a local stream and from the river) is still there, as is the manager's and exciseman's house across the road.

George Willsher's grandson, also called George, still lives in Dundee though the rest of the family has emigrated to the US. He retired a few years ago, finally bringing the shutters down on the family's full-time involvement in the licensed trade. One of his proudest possessions is a 1904 bottle of Glen Coull which, although twice recorked, is otherwise wholly original. It must rate as one of the rarest bottles of whisky in the country.

GLENESK, *Hillside, near Montrose*

This is a distillery with several noted claims to fame. For a start, the buildings lie within a short distance of Kinnabber Junction, the setting for many dramas during the famous London-to-Aberdeen rail races of 1895. Whichever train from London got there first went on ahead to Aberdeen to win the night's run. The distillery has also had more names assigned to it over the years (Highland Esk, North Esk, Montrose and Hillside) than any other. And it is one of a handful of distilleries that started distilling malt, was converted to grain, then converted back to malt again.

Originally a flax mill close to the river North Esk, the plant was converted to a distillery in 1896-97 by a Dundee wine merchant called James Isles who sold it within a year to the delightfully-named Septimus Parsonage, of Mark Lane, London, who named it Highland Esk. Septimus Parsonage and Co Ltd soon ran into cashflow problems and the distillery was taken over in 1899 by J.F. Caille Heddle, who renamed it North Esk.

During World War I it stood idle and was occupied for several years by the army. Part of it was then destroyed by fire and it was bought in 1919 by Thomas Bernard & Co, who used some of the buildings as maltings, operating under the name North Esk Maltings. Then in 1938 Bernards sold the premises to Associated Scottish Distilleries (ASD), made up of long-silent East Coast distilleries acquired and run in the late 1930s by Joseph Hobbs under Train & McIntyre for National Distillers of America.

ASD converted it to grain whisky production and named it Montrose Distillery, but it had hardly been in production a year when war broke out, distilling ground to a halt and the premises became barracks again for the war's duration. Joe Hobbs then sold

Glenesk, Montrose with the operational maltings plant in the distance.

ASD for £38,000 and some whisky options, moved to Fort William, went into cattle ranching and became a hotelier!

After the war, ASD restarted production but regularly faced problems of scarce raw materials, market restrictions and cashflow. In 1954 DCL bought the distillery from its parent company, National Distillers of America, ran it briefly, mothballed it until 1959, then used it as spare grain whisky capacity until 1964. But it was too small a plant to be viable.

In 1964 the distillery was assigned to SMD, who took out the Coffey stills, re-installed pot stills and renamed the place Hillside. As a malt distillery it ran successfully for 16 years until SMD renamed it yet again, this time, Glenesk. The name change did not save it: it was among a dozen or so DCL/SMD locations to be mothballed indefinitely in the mid-1980s. Not that the place became moribund. Far from it. A big maltings was opened beside the distillery in 1968 and was enlarged in 1973 and in subsequent years. Glenesk is now one of the largest maltings in the UK and for several years produced the entire malt requirement for all United Distillers' plants, be they malt or grain. The plant's huge, boxy silo is the biggest landmark for miles around with barley deliveries arriving by both road and rail, the latter via sidings from the nearby Aberdeen-Dundee main line.

The maltings have 24 germination drums, each one holding up to 31 tonnes of barley.

In late 1996, however, DCL sold the entire establishment to Paul's Malts, who are based near Buckie in Banffshire. At that time, too, any remaining distillation equipment was removed from the distillery. In its final distilling years, Glenesk used four stills and was licenced to DCL subsidiary William Sanderson of South Queensferry. Apart from the maltings, the 25-acre site today comprises the former production buildings, acres of low-rise warehousing and offices and a long mill lade that threads its way to the distillery from a weir upriver on the North Esk. In many respects the entire place looks busy and well-kept.

The distillery's single malt, sold by specialist bottlers as either Glenesk or Hillside, is still available and is highly rated. Original bottles of Glenesk are very rare and fetch high prices at auction from collectors. Although far from totally lost, Glenesk will never distil again so its whisky is a real collectors' item.

GLENURY-ROYAL, *Stonehaven*

A distillery with a long and fascinating history, Glenury was opened around 1825 by a local laird and army officer, Captain Barclay, or Barclay Allardice, who was the greatest long-distance walker of his time and a great supporter of prize fighting. He became a living legend by walking 1000 miles in 1000 consecutive hours and won (and lost) huge sums in gambling and gaming. Barnard wrote that he started the distillery in 1836, but other sources show the establishment being run by Barclay-McDonald and Co from 1825-52.

It may have been silent from 1852-58, but in that year the captain sold it to William Ritchie, of Glasgow, who owned and operated it for the rest of the century and probably beyond. It became a limited company in 1890 and remained in the name of William Ritchie until 1938, when it was bought by the famous Joseph Hobbs on behalf of National Distillers of America. They operated it through their Train & McIntyre subsidiary, Associated Scottish Distilleries Ltd.

Like almost all malt distilleries, it was silent for most of the war years, then reopened in 1945-46. Train & McIntyre were bought over by DCL in 1953 and Glenury passed to SMD with the licence going to the DCL subsidiary John Gillon & Co Ltd. The distillery was extensively revamped and enlarged to four pot stills around 1965. It was among a swathe of DCL/SMD distilleries closed or mothballed between 1983 and 1985, the last casks being sent away in 1987. It has stood silent since then, although there were hopes that it might reopen in the early 1990s. These petered out in late 1993 when developers were granted outline planning permission for housing on the distillery's 18-acre site.

Since then, nothing has happened, possibly because of uncertainties in the local housing market and the costs of building on what is a steep and rocky hillside. The distillery is still standing, but all distilling plant has apparently long been removed.

Barnard described Glenury as delightful, washed on its southern walls by the River Cowie, from which it took its process water. On the steep site beneath a big rail viaduct it had three granaries, three malting floors with metal steeps and two peat-fired kilns with wire-cloth floors. The mash tun was 17 feet across with the usual stirring gear and the hot worts passed through two outside underbacks to be cooled by fans driven, unusually, by the water wheel. The worts then flowed into one of six 6,000-gallon washbacks where the froth switchers were also driven by water power, as were most of the pumps.

Glenury-Royal, Stonehaven, 1997

The stillhouse had a 4,000-gallon wash still and a 3,000-gallon low wines still, new wash and low wines chargers, spirit receiver and feints receiver. Barnard noted, too, the huge concrete worm tub, 80 feet long by 12 feet deep, filled by 900 feet of copper worm. All water to the distillery cascaded into the worm tub from an aqueduct and also turned the big water wheel that drove every piece of equipment in the place. The spirit store had a 4,000-gallon vat and a recent addition to the five on-site warehouses holding 10,000 casks was another two-storey warehouse in the town of Stonehaven proper. As with so many distilleries then, Glenury had a cooperage, capenters' shop and various other workshops. Annual output was 132,000 gallons.

The distillery acquired its 'Royal' appellation thanks to the captain's friendship with King William IV, who tried the whisky, liked it and frequently re-ordered it. Many, many years later, this royal connection gave rise to a blend, King William IV, which had liberal quantities of Glenury-Royal in the formula.

At some point, too, the distillery must have had its own vatting and bottling facilities, because for many years in Stonehaven it sold small quantities of two whiskies, Garron and Downie, named after local coastal landmarks, and another blend, Old Angus.

It is still possible to obtain bottles of Glenury-Royal, but it is getting very difficult to find. If you spot a bottle on some off-licence's dusty back shelf, buy it – either to taste a gem of history or to keep as an investment.

GRANDTULLY, *near Aberfeldy*

Grandtully was for much of its 90-year existence the smallest legal distillery in the UK. Even in its halcyon days, output was a paltry 5,000 gallons a year – less than a day's output for some of the big grain or combined distilleries today. It is therefore hardly surprising that it was among those to fold after Lloyd George's notorious tax increase of 1909.

Having said that, Grandtully was probably the nearest thing to an authentic Highland still, with everything done on a small scale by hand. Barnard described it as the smallest and most backward distillery he had ever seen. But to many people, such small-scale, rudimentary, unsophisticated methods were the only way to obtain the true Highland *usque beatha* and it may well have been that the whisky was excellent. Even Barnard said Grandtully's spirit was almost entirely snapped up by all the area bigwigs, including the local MP Donald Currie. What it lacked in quantity it may well have made up in quality.

The distillery was built three miles from Grandtully beside the Cultilloch Burn in the early 1820s and, like all too many distilleries, went through a series of operators. These included Andrew Campbell & Co (1825), John Kennedy & Co (1826), William McFarlane & Co (1827-32), Alexander Duff (1832-33) and John Stewart & Co (1833-34). It then came into the hands of James Thomson, and it remained with the Thomson family virtually from 1837 until its closure around the start of World War I.

Like many farm distilleries, it was part of a large estate, which was quite happy to have a thriving distillery on the estate factor's map. Barnard commented in 1887 that

> *With a view to enlarging the distillery, the architect to the proprietor, Sir Douglas Stewart, took the necessary measurements two years ago, but Mr Thomson is reluctant to disturb the present mode of working or displace the vessels.*

ISLA, *Bridgend, Perth*

From the late 1700s, there was a brewery called Clockserrie or Clockserie at the triangular junction where the Isla and Strathmore roads converged 300 yards from the new bridge across the Tay linking Bridgend and Perth. It was doubtless sited there because of the stream, possibly called Clockserrie, which tumbled down the steep Kinnoull Hill into the same river.

One brewer, Thomas McLean Taylor, fell on hard times and was sequestered in 1839. The brewery on a one acre site was offered for sale by public roup in February, 1840, the press notice saying it was 'suitable as a brewery, distillery or bone mill' and enjoyed a 'good, constant and abundant water supply'.

It was acquired, either then or slightly later, by Alexander Forbes and was operating as Clockserrie Distillery in 1851. It was to stay in the Forbes family for 70 years, first with Alexander, then with his son, John, and with his grandson, Sam, one of two sons born to Mr and Mrs John Forbes in 1872 and 1874.

Exactly when it was renamed Isla is uncertain, but for many years the distillery prospered and expanded, though it was never very large. When visited by Alfred Barnard, annual output was just 30,000 gallons a year. He noted two wash stills and two small spirit stills, their worms cooled by the water of the burn flowing through the site. On the other hand, process water was tapped from the Tay, but well upriver. Isla, noted Barnard, was the only establishment in Scotland he saw lit by Bower lamps, which he extolled as 'second only to electric light'.

The Forbes prospered with the distillery, gradually buying adjacent cottages and houses and eventually moving in to Croft House in Keir Street, an imposing mansion with an Italianate pediment and mock-Serliana window at the front. As Perth grew and prospered, the neighbourhood improved too. Opposite the distillery, behind high walls and amid lush gardens, the Pullars (of laundry and dry-cleaning fame) built an imposing Tayside mansion.

During and after World War I, the Forbes hit hard times and the distillery was bought in 1920 by the Tay Distillery Company Ltd, formed by a consortium of blenders. That went into liquidation in 1923 and a new company, Isla Distillery Ltd, took over the distillery. Fate was no kinder to it than to its predecessors and the distillery ceased operating in 1926. For some years, possibly up to World War II, the warehouses were used for storage and distribution by Wright's Brewery, Perth. Once that ceased, the buildings stood empty and derelict for many years. They were eventually demolished and the triangular site is now a small park with the burn meandering through it, a haven for brown ducks. The Pullars' domain opposite is also gone, replaced by a modern hospital and clinic. Isla Distillery too has vanished.

LOCHSIDE, *Brechin Road, Montrose*

Lochside produced outstanding whisky and the distillery building itself was one of the most striking in Scotland. Yet by the time this book is published the building may well have been flattened and the whisky gone without trace, except among a few aficionados who have managed to hoard a few bottles of Lochside single malt.

Lochside was originally built as a brewery back in the 1890s in the towering Germanic *Brauhaus* style of the era. It stood on the site

Lochside Distillery, 1997. . . soon to be demolished?

of an earlier brewery which is said to have dated back to the 1700s and which drew its water from artesian wells under the site. The new brewery, (later distillery), building covered several acres beside the Montrose Basin and in its heydays, its sheer cream-washed walls and striking tower made it the most visible landmark for miles around.

In its years as a brewery, it was the one location outside Newcastle to produce Newcastle Brown Ale and the brewery's two sea freighters weekly plied the North Sea from Montrose to the Tyne carrying thousands of gallons of the stuff southwards. The brewery, known to everyone as 'Deuchar's' after the family who ran it for many years, eventually closed in the 1950s. In 1956 it was bought by the ubiquitous Joseph Hobbs, who had long cut his links with Associated Scottish Distilleries and now ran the Ben Nevis distillery at Fort William. Hobbs had also acquired the name and trade marks of Glenmavis Distillery at Bathgate (see under Glenmavis), which had stood unused for nearly 40 years after the death around 1910 of the redoubtable John MacNab.

Hobbs combined the two ventures and converted the plant to distilling (though the vast copper-lined beer-brewing vats were left untouched), complete with four pot stills and a 67-foot-high (21m) Coffey still. For a time Lochside was one of a handful of 'combined' distilleries that made malt and grain. Large, bleak modern warehouses sprouted on a greenfield site across the road. After Joe Hobbs died in 1964, his son – also Joe – ran the distillery for nearly a decade, much of it spent seeking a potential buyer.

It was acquired in 1973 by the Spanish firm Destilerias y Crianza, of Madrid, who make Spain's most palatable whisky, DYC (pronounced *Deek*) who were seeking a good source of Scotch malt to blend with their home-produced spirits. DYC mothballed the Coffey still and focused all production on malt whisky. For nigh on 20 years, Lochside was one of Scotland's most industrious distilleries. It produced malt whisky for Spain and for the blenders and also vatted and bottled various whiskies on site on its own production line.

However, Lochside became a victim of the rationalisation that swept the world drinks industry in the late 1980s and early 1990s. DYC were acquired by Domecq, the sherry group, which in turn was taken over by the Canadian firm Hiram Walker and eventually by Allied Distillers. As a result, Allied finished up with a far larger portfolio of distilleries than they could use. Several of these distilleries were put up for sale and those which could not be sold as going concerns were offered to developers.

In such circumstances, it was perhaps inevitable that Lochside should draw the short straw. Its delicate malt, probably among the best in Scotland, was relatively unknown even in malt-drinking circles. The plant, although good enough in the 1960s, was obsolescent. It did not stand in illustrious Speyside but in unfashionable Montrose. Its distilling pedigree went back barely 35 years. Lastly, it stood on a good urban site slap beside two main roads and with several acres of land to develop. Once the place was advertised, potential bidders were soon on the scene.

It took almost five years after distilling ceased in April 1992 for all casks in bond to be moved to Spain or otherwise disposed of. A skeleton staff under manager Charles Sharpe stayed on to oversee all the necessary work but all staff bar the manager departed in late 1996. The site was handed to the developers in February 1997 and demolition work was due to start soon after. Local conservationists campaigned to have the great Brauhaus tower preserved, only to find it did not even have listed status.

During its final years the distillery disposed of several thousand cases of whisky, both Lochside malt and the distillery's own blend, Sandy Macnab, which had been bottled on site, largely for export. These were bought by local and enthusiast buyers. Many who have sampled Sandy Macnab, especially at export strength, rate it as one of the best blends to come out of Scotland.

NORTH PORT, *Brechin*

North Port holds a special place in my affections. I was born in the street where it stood and its high brick chimney and very visible lightning conductor were the dominant landmarks to be seen from our front windows. One early childhood memory is of walking past men shovelling steaming draff into carts and closing my nose to the hot, overpowering smell that poured out of the place. Aged a bold four, I asked my granny what they did in this forbidding building. She said: 'They make whisky. It's a drink and it doesn't taste nice.'

I remember thinking even then what a daft bunch grown-ups were to have this great, hot, bustling edifice churning out a drink that did not taste nice. I only found out when I was much older that granny's view on whisky reflected her good Victorian upbringing. One sweet sherry on Christmas morning tended to be the sum total of her year's imbibing. However, her quaint reply planted the seed of curiosity that, 50 years later, has lead to this book.

North Port Distillery, 1993, prior to demolition

North Port first opened its doors in 1820 under the Townhead Distillery Company, launched by the three Guthrie brothers, David, John and Alexander of the noted divine Dr Thomas Guthrie. Five years later it became Guthrie, Martin & Co, which operated the distillery for just under a century, becoming limited in 1893. Annual output was around 100,000 gallons in the late 19th century. In 1922 the company was bought by DCL and W.H. Holt Ltd, wound up and the distillery passed to SMD. They duly closed it from 1928 until 1937. Except for the wartime enforced silent season, it then operated for 46 years until it was mothballed by SMD in 1983.

After that it became obvious that re-opening was not a viable proposition. The main chimney was demolished brick by brick in the mid-1980s; the cooling pond, fed by the Den Burn, was filled in and a funeral parlour built on it. The bonded warehouse was also emptied. After years of on-off planning applications, it was finally demolished in 1994 and a Presto supermarket and car park built on the site. However, a small decorative wall and pediment were built on the site of the old chimney with a plaque marking the passing of the plant.

North Port whisky all went for blending although it can still be obtained from the specialist bottlers or occasionally found in hotel bars which pride themselves on keeping every malt in the book. The connoisseur Wallace Milroy describes it as having 'a rather sharp, pronounced aroma, almost like a pickle' and advises it to be taken 'pre-dinner, preferably with water'. My own memories of it are that it had almost a touch of Islay – most unusual in such an East coast whisky.

STRATHDEE, *Aberdeen*

Strathdee was the smallest of Aberdeen's three notable distilleries, but it managed to outlive its two bigger rivals by some 30 years. It was established in 1821 by Henry Ogg, who already operated the city's Ferryhill Brewery (which may well have become the Bon-Accord Distillery in 1855). His son, also Henry, eventually took over the business and ran it until 1895, when it was acquired by another Aberdeen businessman, David Walker, who ran it for a further 20 years. In 1915, Strathdee Distillery Co was formed, which was acquired in 1920 by Robertson and Co, which in turn was swallowed in 1925 by the Glasgow merchants Train & McIntyre, who became part of National Distillers of America in the 1930s.

Through Train McIntyre and the efforts of the talented Joseph Hobbs, NDA acquired a swathe of distilleries in the interwar years, including Bruichladdich on Islay, Benromach near Forres, Glenkinchie at Pencaitland and the East-coast distilleries of Fettercairn, Royal Glenury and Glenesk, near Montrose. Some of these survive, but Strathdee was less lucky. Like all malt distilleries it was mothballed during World War II, but was not reopened in 1945.

Barnard described it externally as a low, old-fashioned place, though he admitted the equipment was as good as any he had seen. It produced 50,000-55,000 gallons a year, virtually all sent for blending or export to agents in Leith and Liverpool. It used mains water for processing and a local stream, now totally forgotten and culverted, for cooling. Just when it was demolished in the postwar era is unclear, but the site is now a garage and car showroom. Like Bon Accord, Strathdee has disappeared virtually without trace.

STRONACHIE, *Forgandenny*

Stronachie is a fascinating distillery. It was built in the 1890s by Messrs Alexander and Macdonald at the top of a forsaken glen in Forgandenny parish, just north of the Perth-Kinross county line – so its product could be called Highland Malt. It stood between the hills of Slungie and Dochrie on an unnumbered road that toiled through the Ochils from Forgandenny to Milnathort. Getting raw materials to, and barrels of spirit from Stronachie was a major task, especially as Milnathort rail station was six miles away along roads that were poor at the best of times and almost impassable in bad weather.

Yet built it was and it operated for nearly 30 years. Not that it did not have its ups and downs. Alexander Macdonald sold it in 1907 to Sir James Calder, one of the industry's major figures, whose company owned Bo'ness grain distillery. After World War I, Sir James also acquired Dalwhinnie, Glendullan and Auchinblae and eventually sold all four and various other assets to DCL in 1926. The distillery was transferred to the St James Export Company Ltd which closed it down towards the end of the decade.

Stronachie held a special niche in Sir James Calder's affections. His period home, Ledlanet, was only a few miles away and he regularly visited his isolated pride and joy. Like his father, Sir James was one of the giant characters of the industry, frequently being seen chauffeured everywhere in his splendid car. But he and his company were eventually brought low by the industry's unending decline of fortunes from 1900-30. Stronachie is thought to have been dismantled around 1930, though the buildings were only finally razed in the 1950s.

Stronachie has other claims to fame. From early on, transport between the distillery and Milnathort rail yard was by a steam traction engine pulling solid-wheeled trailers. Damage to the roads was enormous, protest about it often intense. The matter was resolved in the 1920s when a five-mile narrow-guage railway was built from Stronachie to Seggie (or Meikle Seggie) Farm, run by the Syme family about two miles from Milnathort.

The railway, the longest private distillery line in Britain, was built on an embankment east of the existing road. Trains were pulled by a specially-ordered petrol-engined Guy tractor whose solid-tyred road wheels straddled the narrow-guage line and ran on two hardcore bands on either side. To guide it, the front of the tractor was bolted to a bogie that ran on the rails and lifted the front wheels clear of the ground.

On arrival at Seggie, the tractor was unhooked from train and bogie, barrels were rolled onto road-going trailers and the tractor pulled these to Milnathort station. The system was reversed to take empty barrels, coal and other raw materials from Milnathort to Stronachie. Two obvious questions remain unanswered. Why was the distillery line not extended to Milnathort to obviate the cumbersome changeover at Seggie? And what happened to the railway after the distillery closed?

Remnants of old distilling plant litter the site at Stronachie Distillery

The tractor was brought to Stronachie, then was driven, serviced and repaired by a long-haired Devon man, Bill Pascoe, and his assistant, a Yorkshireman called Wragg. Pascoe was unmarried and, like many men at the distillery, had a motorbike. He regularly roared down to Giacopazzi's chip shop in Milnathort and bought a vast quantity of chips which he stuffed inside his leather jacket before roaring back to Stronachie. The railway also held a fascination for the two young lads at the distillery, manager's son James Stephen and his pal Tom Watson. In the May-August silent season, they would push the little rail wagons to the top of the pass and roll down to the distillery, reaching speeds of 40-50mph and often derailing at the sharp turn where the line curved its way around the distillery walls.

Another regular of the Stronachie road was the young errand boy from Milnathort grocers, Tyndall McLellan. Weekly or fortnightly he would pedal uphill to take the shopping orders from the five or so distillery cottages, the exciseman's house and the bothy. He would take the orders and money, the goods being delivered two days later by Tyndall McLellan's deliveryman, John Finlay, often with his son Bob on a flat horsewagon pulled by two Clydesdales with the boxes of groceries protected from the weather under a tarpaulin.

Before the tractor-railway system was introduced, whisky barrels were carted to Milnathort by wily old Bain, the horseman. Like many a man in that particular job, he had his own sweet way of getting a sly drop of the cratur. On a lonely stretch of road, he would drill a small hole in the top of a barrel, stick in a straw and suck up some whisky, then pop a tiny wooden bung in the hole and hammer it tight. Everyone knew he did it, but everyone seemed prepared to look the other way.

Records of what Stronachie looked like are scant. It was an imposing enough edifice set in a square with separate bonded warehouses, a millwheel and a high round brick chimney. The distillery stood east of the road on flat ground while the cottages stood west of the road on the steep slope of Slungie Hill. Process water came from a Chapel Burn tributary, dammed, channelled and finally piped. Peats were locally dug by distillery staff and barley came both from local farmers (who were Calder tenants) and from overseas. Children went to school two miles north at Path of Condie, under the awesome tawse-wielding Miss Macdonald, though she was later replaced by the popular Miss Pirie. Path of Condie also had a small village hall – the nearest social centre to Stronachie. The distillery's great social event was the annual dance in the loft of the malt barn, complete with band, buffet and doubtless a touch of the house best.

Sadly, virtually everything has gone at Stronachie. Only a few low walls and lines of stones bear witness to its once great presence. Even people who remember it well say they now fail to spot its remnants until they have almost driven past. The obliteration is total. Only the name remains.

Central And Lothian

This is very interesting historic territory. Although hardly any distilleries are to be found near the banks of the River Forth today, this area – particularly around Alloa – was in many ways the birthplace of commercial distilling in Scotland. The two early whisky dynasties, the Haigs and the Steins, started their first distilleries here and John Jameson, that giant of Irish distilling, originally emigrated from Alloa to Dublin.

Losses here are a mixture of grain and malt distilleries. If scant attention tends to be paid to the former in most whisky books, it is because they have always been seen as giant industrial plants churning out millions of gallons of raw spirits, devoid of the identity and character of malt distilleries. To draw an analogy from wine, they are seen as producers of dull bulk plonk while the malt distilleries produce the chateau-bottled grands crus. Although most grain spirit goes into blended whisky, increasing quantities are today distilled to make gin and vodka or alcohol for the perfume and solvent industries. In the late 1930s, millions of gallons were used as automotive fuel. With the need to find a replacement for fossil fuels now becoming crucial, industrial alcohol produced from cheap biomass raw materials may one day be a growth industry and Scotland may remain a big source of fuel long after North Sea oil is a distant memory.

In addition to the names listed below, two early distilleries in the area deserve special mention – Kennetpans and Kilbagie, both near Alloa. Both were built around 1777 by the Stein family and were among the first large, licensed pot-still distilleries in Scotland and were the sources of early bulk exports of whisky to England. Kennetpans was closed in 1825, though its ruins can still be seen

The remains of the once great Kennetpans Distillery with the rotting remains of the wharves and landing stages where boats once loaded spirit bound for London and beyond

today. Kilbagie was a pioneering plant for Coffey-still production with output starting in August 1845. As with many other distilleries, including Seggie at Guard Bridge in Fife, switching from pot to patent stills was no guarantee of success: Kilbagie ceased distilling in 1852, became a fertiliser plant in 1860 and a paper mill in 1874.

Other grain closures here include Glenochil at Menstrie, Carsebridge at Alloa and Cambus and Strathmore at Cambus. The first three were among the five founding distilleries of DCL in 1877. Glenochil ceased distilling decades ago to become a yeast plant and the main laboratories of DCL and later United Distillers. Carsebridge stopped distilling in the early 1980s and was part-demolished in 1992. Strathmore brewery at Cambus was converted to distilling in 1957-58, made malt for two years, then converted to grain. It too closed in recent years as did its huge neighbour, Cambus, mothballed in September, 1993.

Today UD is concentrating all grain production on Cameron Bridge, at Windygates in Fife, and at Port Dundas in Glasgow. Incredibly, Clackmannanshire's four great grain distilleries have now all gone.

One notable recent malt closure in Central Scotland was Rosebank at Falkirk, one of just three distilleries remaining which still used triple distillation and whose single malt was, and is, acclaimed by many enthusiasts as the best of the Lowland malts. There are rumours in the trade that Rosebank's days may not yet be over but at present the future looks a little bleak.

Bankier, Denny, Stirlingshire (1827-1928)

Bo'ness (1813-1925)

Cambus, Tullibody, Clackmannanshire (1806-1993)

Carsebridge, Alloa, Clackmannanshire (1799-1983)

Glenfoyle (*aka* Dasherhead, Gargunnock, Westerkepp), Gargunnock, near Stirling (1826-1923)

Glenmavis, Bathgate, Lothian (1795-1910)

Glenochil, Menstrie, Clackmannanshire (1746-1929)

Kirkliston (1795-1900 approx)

Rosebank, Camelon, Falkirk (1798-1993)

St Magdalene, Linlithgow, Lothian (1798-1983)

Strathmore (*aka* North of Scotland), Cambus, Clackmannanshire (1957-c1982)

BANKIER, *Denny, Stirlingshire*

Bankier is one of some six distilleries built close to the Forth-Clyde canal, the others being mainly at Port Dundas in Glasgow and at Falkirk. Originally a corn mill between Castlecary and Denny, it was converted to distilling in 1827 by Paisley man Daniel MacFarlane, acquiring the name Bankier Distillery Company in 1838. The company was reformed a decade later and, despite many changes and alterations, kept that name until 1925. Company and distillery were acquired by James Risk in 1878 and by James Buchanan and Co Ltd in 1903. It was finally passed to DCL in 1925 and closed in 1928. However, the maltings stayed in use until 1971 and the warehouses until the late 1980s. Its last remains were finally demolished around 1990.

It was visited by Barnard, who portrayed it as a thriving place, very clean and efficient, spread out over six pleasant, then almost rural, acres. Moray and Angus barley arrived by barge and was shifted by horse-drawn tram wagons to the barley lofts. Coal too

Bankier Distillery, 1966 (John R.Hume)

arrived by barge and peats (dug from the Cumbernauld moors when Cumbernauld was but a hamlet) rolled in by cart. Process water and water power came from the Doups Stream, which touched the site on its downhill rush to the Bonny River. The buildings were low and scattered, with two high chimneys (75ft and 100ft) the main landmarks. In the 1880s it claimed to make 'Highland-type' malt whisky and had a large, 6,500-gallon wash still and two smaller spirit stills, whose total spirit output was 150,000-180,000 gallons a year.

Uphill from the production buildings were seven warehouses, with a total capacity of 4,500 casks, or well over 200,000 gallons. It was a classic wholly-integrated, self-sufficient distillery with everything on site – peat barn, engine house, two cooperages, two huge spent wash tanks and a draff pit. Like many distilleries of the era it also had its own pig farm, with 100 draff-fed porkers in sties around a large central feeding yard.

A quarter mile uphill stood Bankier House, which at the time of Barnard's visit was James Risk's residence, complete with swan-topped miniature lake and manicured lawns and gardens. Manager's house and employees' cottages stood on the main road opposite the distillery's eastern gate. It was a scene that was not to last. Today every last vestige is gone.

BO'NESS, *Bo'ness, West Lothian*

One of a handful of distilleries that producd both malt and grain whisky, Bo'ness was the bedrock of the great but now long-gone Calder empire. It was one of two distilleries which opened in the West Lothian port in the early 1800s. One stood in South Street and was operated by the Grieve brothers from 1817 until 1842, when the surviving brother died and the modest firm went bust.

The other distillery was decidedly more successful. It opened in 1813 at Pan's Braes, overlooking the Forth, as a partnership between Messrs Tod, Padon and Vannen (also spelled Vannan or Vannon) which held until 1829, after which only the Vannens remained. They improved the distillery and ran it until 1873, when it was bought by James Calder and Company, who extended the works, dismantled the pot stills, installed Coffey stills and converted it to grain output in 1876. It was initially called Bo'ness Distillery Company, but was incorporated as James Calder and Co Ltd in 1894. Along with almost the entire Calder empire, it was sold to John Dewar in 1921, passed to DCL in 1925 and closed down. The warehouses were used by DCL until recent times but now the entire place has been demolished.

In its late-Victorian heydays, Bo'ness covered several acres, had a 700ft frontage and a direct rail link to the harbour, whence wagon upon wagon of seaborne imported maize was daily shunted to the distillery. Barley came in also by rail, as did vast quantities of coal. However, being a grain distillery, no peats were required.

Across the road stood two vast bonded warehouses with a total capacity of 5,000 barrels. Output from the single huge, round-the-clock Coffey still was 870,000 gallons a year, almost all of which went to the blenders. The plant also became one of Britain's main yeast factories, producing vast quantities for the bulk-baking and brewing industries. It was said to be packed in special conical bags containing (in those far-off pre-metric days) seven, 14 and 28lb respectively. Around 1912, yeast output was 50 tons a week, plus 300 tons of draff.

Because of the different raw materials and processes used in making grain whisky, Bo'ness and all grain distilleries produced slightly different by-products. Coffey stills isolate small quantities of fusel oil, roughly one gallon to every 500 of spirit. Initially regarded almost as a waste product, fusel oil saw its market grow spectacularly in World War I when it was used to make many varnishes and aircraft 'dope'. Other by-products were grain draff (the shiny orange husks of maize) and 'spent wash'. This was different to pot ale and contained quantities of grist and starchy material. This was allowed to settle in vast dreg tanks or dreg ponds outside. The top fluid was gradually run off and the gooey dregs left in the tank were increasingly dried, pelleted, bagged and sold as livestock feed.

CAMBUS, *Tullibody, Clackmannanshire*

A distillery that dates back to the times when bulk commercial distilling was in its infancy, Cambus enjoyed a long and distinguished history and was among the first distilleries in Scotland to convert to grain whisky production. In 1806, one John Mowbray or Moubray converted a derelict mill on the River Devon, just before it joined the Forth, to a pot-still malt distillery. He was a go-ahead man. He formally registered the business in 1813, gained title to the ground in 1823 and converted Cambus to grain distilling in 1836, possibly with an early Coffey still or similar apparatus. The business then passed to his ambitious son, James, who expanded grain output, built up a herd of 450 cattle on the draff and other residue, then overreached himself and was sequestrated in 1843.

Cambus, seen from across the River Devon

His son Robert took over, installed a bigger grain still 'similar to Coffey's' in 1851 and eventually made Cambus one of the largest grain plants in Scotland. Under Robert, Cambus became a founder member of DCL in 1877. In 1882 it bought Cambus Old Brewery to enlarge the distillery's malting capacity. Barnard visited in 1886 and extolled the distillery's bustling eight-acre site where 'rail sidings ran to all the principal warehouses'.

Grain came in by rail and from a nearby wharf on the Forth. Four steam engines and a vast water wheel powered by the River Devon drove all the plant machinery. There were two huge Coffey stills and a third stillhouse for yet another was under construction. All process water then came from the River Devon, but in later years it was sourced from Lossburn Reservoir in the Ochils while reducing water came from Loch Turret. In 1886, annual output was nigh on a million gallons and the distillery's six vast warehouses held, at the time Barnard called, more than 17,000 casks containing 1.4 million gallons. The total warehouse capacity was 25,000 casks and more than two million gallons. Cambus was in the big league.

Interestingly, among the excisemen at Cambus around the time of Barnard's visit was a young man called Philip Snowden, who had just joined the customs service and years later was to become Chancellor of the Exchecquer in the first Labour Government.

Cambus, thanks to its strong position in DCL, weathered most of the storms that beset the industry between 1900 and 1914 until, in that year, disaster struck. On the gale-blasted night of 24 September, fire broke out in the maltings and grain stores and eventually engulfed most of the distillery. Only the bonded warehouses and their precious contents were spared. As a result the distillery closed and did not reopen until 1938.

In the intervening years, it did not lie totally idle. It was used as bonded warehousing and extra maltings for Carsebridge. Then, amid the heady late-1930s upsurge in demand, DCL decided to demolish the fire-gutted shell of Old Cambus and build anew at a cost of £275,000. Production started in December 1937 and the distillery was formally reopened in January 1938. A host of projects – including Saladin maltings and a rectification plant – were planned for Cambus, but the outbreak of war put them on ice. In the post-war years, Cambus saw the installation of the rectifier around 1952, a carbon dioxide processing plant in 1953, 18 warehouses between 1955 and 1957, a cattle feed drying plant in 1964 and a dark grains plant in 1982. That year the nearby Strathmore grain distillery, which had recently closed, was bought to allow future expansion.

Yet, amazingly, this big and indomitable distillery was closed by United Distillers on 14 September 1993 – almost eight decades after its fire-enforced closure of 1914 – and grain production concentrated at Cameron Bridge, 30 miles away in Fife and at Port Dundas in Glasgow. Cambus still stands and is being used as a cask-filling centre and for bonded warehousing. However, it looks as if its distilling days are gone for good.

CARSEBRIDGE, *Alloa*

Each of the big Clackmannan distilleries was linked in its early years to one family – Cambus to the Mowbrays, Glenochil to the McNabs and Carsebridge to the Balds, who stayed at the helm for several generations. Carsebridge, occasionally listed as Kerse Bridge, was established between 1799 and 1804 by John Bald in a then rural setting a mile north-east of Alloa. It was listed under John Bald & Co from 1813, though it seems to have been a partnership with his eldest son, Robert, who inherited the distillery on his father's death in 1844. A year later he sold it to his brother, also John, who came back north from Liverpool and became the firm's driving force.

In 1851-52 he switched the distillery from malt to grain production by installing a Coffey still and he was to expand Carsebridge hugely in the following decades. Carsebridge was also a founder member of DCL in 1877 – and the decision to join earned John the nickname of 'Politic Bald'. He died some time in the early 1880s.

When Barnard visited in 1886, in terms of output it was the second or third-largest distillery in Scotland and was managed by John's nephew, Colonel Bald Harvey. Barnard portrayed it as a busy ten-acre establishment whose two vast granaries had some 3,000 tons of grain stockpiled. There were four kilns, one an Armstrong of Belfast patent kiln which was 70 feet high.

The mash house was vast with seven tuns, more than in any other distillery he visited. One was brand new, 26 feet in diameter and eight feet deep, that stood on cast-iron pillars so that farmers' draff carts could roll right underneath and be filled directly through a sluice from the tun. There were also six brewing tanks, two each

Grain silos and maltings at Carsebridge Distillery. These are soon to be demolished

in 10,000, 15,000 and 20,000-gallon sizes. The worts, cooled in refrigerators high in the stillhouse, then went to one of 25 washbacks arranged, said Barnard, like opposing armies: 13 held 10,000 gallons each, four held 20,000, seven held 30,000 and one monster some 40,000 gallons. Had they all been full at one time, nearly half-a-million gallons of worts would have been fermenting to wash!

In two stillhouses separated by iron doors stood the two Coffey stills, the wash pumped to them by several three-throw pumps from a wash charger that was 80 feet square and occupied one entire stillhouse floor area. Elsewhere stood eight vast boilers and no fewer than 14 steam engines totalling 400 hp. Smoke from all the boilers converged into two chimneys, 100 and 140 feet high. The spirit store had four vats the total capacity of which was just under 23,000 gallons. Annual output ranged from 1.4 to 1.7 million gallons, all of it grain spirit.

Barnard also mentioned 12 large bonded warehouses, a six-man cooperage, stabling for 13 horses, a Shand and Mason fire engine and 44 fire plugs and all the usual workshops, offices and other paraphernalia. There were 150 employees at the plant, 40 of whom were in the distillery fire brigade. All water came from the Gartmorn Dam reservoir, one mile distant, which still stands today although the distillery closed in 1983 and has since been partly demolished and converted to other uses.

One signal weakness of Carsebridge in the 1880s was that it had no direct transport links, other than road. There was no canal or private rail siding (although a siding was built later) and all maize and other cereals had to be laboriously hauled from Alloa harbour, some distance away, to the distillery by sealed horse carts which carried not much more than a ton per trip.

Carsebridge's years under DCL are relatively unchronicled. It was transferred in 1966 from DCL to its subsidiary, Scottish Grain Distillers, a third Coffey still was installed and a dark grains plant added some years later. In the wake of the downturn of the early 1980s, the plant was closed in 1983.

Most of the warehouses have since been demolished and their site donated to the local development authority as a business park. Some buildings are still used by United Distillers for storage and other purposes and UD's technical and biotechnology centre is situated there. Of the distilling side, virtually nothing is left.

GLENFOYLE, *Gargunnock, near Stirling*

For two decades in the early 19th century, the tiny Stirlingshire village of Gargunnock boasted two distilleries, Easterkepp and Westerkepp, linked to the one farm and standing cheek-by-jowl. Although the village lies in the centre of Scotland, four miles due west of Stirling and looking down on the River Forth, it stands north of the famous 'Highland Line' and its whisky was classed as Highland malt. A single distillery, Kepp, was established in 1795 by David Cassells (or Cassils), whose son John took over in 1813. In 1825, he split the place into two distilleries, Easterkepp and Westerkepp, but financially overstretched himself and was sequestrated the following year.

Westerkepp was sold to one Robert Bell, who promptly sold it on to Andrew Chrystal and John McNee. John Cassells retained Easterkepp and struggled on with it until he was sequestrated again in 1842. Westerkepp fared better, changing its name at some point to Glenfoyle with the Chrystal family operating it until 1868 or later. It was put up for sale or let in July 1870 and was eventually acquired by James Johnstone, who already operated Paisley's Glenpatrick distillery. He did not last long and in 1880 the distillery

Dasherhead Farm, parts of which were once Glenfoyle Distillery

was bought by James Calder, who owned Bo'ness and was to buy a swathe of distilleries in the boom times of the late Victorian era.

It was enlarged by the Calders, the company was renamed the Glenfoyle Distillery Company and as such survived the difficult years from 1900-20. In 1921 Calders were bought out by Perth-based John Dewar and Sons, who closed the distillery in 1923. The site and remaining warehouse were acquired by Glasgow blenders Brodie Hepburn Ltd and used as a bonded warehouse to store the output of Tullibardine, 20 miles away at Blackford, which Brodie Hepburn restored and reopened in 1953. Both the Glenfoyle warehouse and Tullibardine were sold to the Invergordon group in 1971. Glenfoyle has been totally disused since the 1970s, with part of the distillery complex now a private residence. Other parts of the distillery buildings still stand and the curious, or informed, passer-by driving along the A811 will find hints and vestiges of its distilling history.

 GLENMAVIS, *Bathgate, West Lothian*

Glenmavis was unusual in several respects. It was a classic rural malt distillery, but located in the industrial central belt rather than the Highlands or on the East coast. After several owners failed to make headway with it in the early 1800s, it was bought in 1831 by John MacNab who operated it virtually until it closed around 1910. Uniquely among malt distilleries, it used a Coffey still – installed in

1855 – which must have been the most underused item of plant in the whole Scotch whisky industry. It had a known output of 2,000 gallons of spirit per 22-hour day, yet Glenmavis production in the mid-1880s was only 80,000 gallons a year.

Why Glenmavis had a Coffey still is a mystery. However, I suspect – though I have been unable to obtain any confirmation – that John MacNab was offered the Coffey still at a knockdown price by one of the big industrial distillers, such as the Haigs or the Steins. In the 1840s, several big distilleries installed Coffey stills, not all of which were successful. It also lead to overcapacity and the occasional mothballing and shutdown. Mr MacNab may have been offered the used still and its ancillary equipment for much less than the cost of two new pot stills. At any rate, it was installed in 1855 and seems to have been successfully used for well over half a century.

The rambling distillery buildings lay on a steeply-sloping site north of Bathgate beside a burn which turned an overshot water-wheel and provided cooling water. However, process water came from two reservoirs, at Castle Hill and Sunnyside. There were maltings both at the distillery and in Bathgate town, with warehouses for a total of 2,000 casks on the two sites as well.

Barnard found the distillery, Coffey still apart, somewhat rustic and old-fashioned, with the worts being fan-cooled in an era when everyone had a Morton's refrigerator. However, old John MacNab seems to have been quite a character, selling his whisky at home and overseas, much of it bottled under his own label, 'MacNab's Celebrated Glenmavis Dew'. He kept a 65-head herd of cattle, feeding them on the draff. The distillery had 16 staff, three excisemen and a squad of seven horses and carts that carried barley, malt, coal, peat and barrels daily between Bathgate station and the distillery.

It closed shortly before World War I, but the company did not go wholly out of existence. The entrepreneur Joseph Hobbs bought the MacNab name, possibly after World War II, opened Lochside Distillery in Montrose in 1957-58 under the name MacNab Distilleries Ltd and marketed a blended whisky called Sandy MacNab. The ruined remnants of Glenmavis were pulled down a few years ago and a smart residential cul-de-sac now stands on the steep site. Old Glenmavis House, long linked to the distillery, today still stands amid fine gardens and the nearest pub has a mirror extolling MacNab's whisky in pride of place in the bar.

GLENOCHIL, *Menstrie, Clackmannanshire*

This distillery is a bit of an enigma. In theory there should be abundant information about it, but in practice such information is hard to come by. According to Barnard, it started in 1746 – the year of the Battle of Culloden – yet it has not been possible to confirm that fact from other sources. For a century its development was obscure, but in 1846 a Coffey still was installed and the plant converted from malt to grain distilling and, as the cliché goes, it never looked back. The switch to grain production in 1846 was done by the McNab Brothers – no relation to the MacNabs of Glenmavis. The company still bore their names 40 years later when Barnard came to call. It was one of the founding distilleries of DCL and remained in the DCL fold from then on.

Barnard described its location in great detail, recording that it was on the banks of the Devon, four miles from Tillicoultry, five from Stirling and 13 from the celebrated Rumbling Bridge. The distillery's tall chimney stacks were, he noted, the most dominant landmarks in the surrounding plain. For a rural distillery, Glenochil

One of the few remaining Victorian buildings at Glenochil, originally probably a grain store

was big. It had three vast barley stores in buildings 120 feet by 60, three commensurate malting floors and a malt kiln 24 feet by 45 floored with perforated steel plates. There were 11 grain stores, each 120 feet by 80, all fronting onto a private rail siding. The maize or other unmalted cereals were dried in a vast hot air kiln (no peat was used in grain distilling) and, after milling, the maize grist was fed into a 12-foot deep, 20-foot diameter mash tun. This emptied its worts into a second, 30-foot diameter mash tun underneath to mix with malt grist that catalysed the conversion of starch to sugar.

Unusually, the lower tun was emptied by cranes into two underbacks, each 24 feet by 12, from which the worts were pumped via cooling tanks and three big Morton's refrigerators to the washbacks or fermenting tuns. No sizes or capacities were given for these, but the stillroom wash charger held 30,000 gallons, so the washbacks must have been in the same league. The charger fed two large Coffey stills virtually round the clock and the cooled spirit poured into two 5,000-gallon spirit receivers.

After dilution and casking, the spirit was rolled to one of seven bonded warehouses covering three acres, all under one roof. Again, no warehouse sizes or capacities were given, but output was given as a million gallons a year, putting Glenochil among the top half-dozen distilleries in Scotland. The distillery also boasted seven pairs of milling stones, five steam engines, six boilers and the standard array of carpenters', coopers' and engineers' workshops. There were 100 people on the payroll, plus seven excise officers.

During the 1870s, Glenochil was among the first grain plants to go into so-called German yeast production and it became an important and lucrative sideline. One and a quarter centuries later, Glenochil is still a yeast plant. Although it survived the industry's many problems in the early decades of the 20th century, distilling eventually ceased in 1929. Yeast production continued and for years it was the site of DCL's main research laboratories and testing centre. Today many buildings have been demolished and much, if not all, research work has been transferred to United Distillers' technical centre at Carsebridge in Alloa. The yeast manufacturing plant is now operated by the Quest division of the Anglo-Dutch giant, Unilever. Most of Glenochil is now gone and it is without doubt a lost distillery.

KIRKLISTON, *West Lothian*

Kirkliston was one of the original grain distilleries which with five others in 1877 formed the mighty Distillers Company Limited, that was to dominate the industry for more than a century. It was also quite a fascinating distillery in its own right, with three ingenious features to it.

It was established, possibly under the name Lambsmiln, in 1795 and over its first 30 years had three owners and operators. It was bought in 1825 by Andrew Stein of the Stein distilling dynasty, who installed one of the first Stein continuous-output malt triple-stills in the plant. It was not a success and he was sequestered in 1831. Distilling resumed the following year under the name Patent Distillery Co, which lasted one year. Over the next two decades, it passed to Andrew Philp, Ralph Strachan, Buchanan & Co and finally to John Stewart & Co, who took over in 1855. Under the Buchanans in 1850 the Stein stills had been pulled out and Kirkliston had returned to simple pot distilling. Stewarts reversed the process yet again, installed a Coffey still and converted Kirkliston largely to grain distilling.

Kirkliston Distillery, 1993

When Barnard visited it in the 1880s, it was a combined distillery, making pot-still malt as well as grain, though the latter accounted for the larger proportion of the 700,000-gallon-a-year output. Barnard was impressed by three things at Kirkliston. One was an overhead enclosed conveyor system that carried grain and barley to the many lofts. It was outside, above roof height, yet totally enclosed in a big box duct made of iron sheeting. Such overhead ducting systems are two-a-penny today, but in those days it was a whisky industry first. Second was the ingenious, yet totally obvious, idea of cooling the worts in pipes running in the mill lade, saving the need for refrigerators. Third was the idea of running all the waste water down a big sewage pipe to the Firth of Forth. It would have been an impossibly expensive project had it been done from scratch – but they laid it alongside the railway track that ran from Kirkliston down to South Queensferry in a deep cutting, paying the railway an annual fee for the privilege.

Kirkliston ceased distilling sometime early this century but was used for many years by DCL to make yeast and other products linked to brewing and distilling. A high red-brick building was added in the 1930s. DCL eventually closed the plant but it has been in operation again for many years under its new owners, Malt Products (UK) Ltd, who make yeast, malt extract, home-brew kits and other malt-linked products at the plant. Kirkliston too has a near-neighbour strongly linked to whisky and Scottish tradition – the liqueur-makers Drambuie. In that respect, Kirkliston is still very much on the drinkers' map.

ROSEBANK, *Camelon, Falkirk*

A remarkable distillery with an excellent reputation, Rosebank was, in its later years, saddled with one particular problem. It stood in unglamorous Falkirk beside the long-closed Forth-Clyde Canal. After its closure many a malt drinker was to lament that had it stood in open countryside in a tourist area, it might never have been shut down.

There are records of a distillery on the site as early as 1798, run by the Stark Brothers. Also James Robertson ran a distillery (either the same one or with the same name) from 1817-19. Across the canal stood Camelon Distillery, which started in the late-18th century and was run by one John Stark, one of the Stark brothers, from 1827 until his death in 1836. It was taken over by the Gunns, either Thomas Gunn or his father, who ran it until 1861 when they were sequestrated.

In the meantime, in 1840, the Gunns sold or leased the Camelon maltings (across the canal on what is the Rosebank site) to James Rankine, who started Rosebank and was to run it, as later would his sons, for several decades. In a strange reverse of fortunes, when Camelon went to the wall in 1861, Rankine bought it. He

The vast worm tubs outside Rosebank Distillery, 1997

demolished much of it but kept the maltings – though one source says the site was razed and new maltings built. Whatever the case, the maltings stayed in use until 1968.

Rosebank flourished under the Rankines. The distillery was enlarged in 1845, rebuilt in 1864-65, the company name was changed to Rosebank Distillery Ltd in 1894 with a share capital of £120,000 and it was a founding company of SMD (Scottish Malt Distillers) in 1914. It was silent from 1917-19 – as were most distilleries – but it was one of a handful of malt distilleries which operated throughout World War II. In all its operational years, it distilled only malt whisky and for decades its output was exclusively triple-distilled.

During his visit in 1886, Barnard noted the distillery stood on two sites, connected by a bridge across the canal. All malt made in the ex-Camelon maltings was duly kiln-dried, bagged and carted across the bridge to the distillery proper. There it was hoisted to the malt deposit, ground to grist and fed into the 16-foot diameter by six-foot deep mash tun with hot water from three heating coppers. The worts were cooled by two consecutive cooler systems, the latter an early Morton's refrigerator, before being pumped to one of eight washbacks, each holding 3,500 gallons. Wash would then be pumped to the three pot stills, two wash stills holding 3,000 gallons and a 1,500-gallon spirit still, flanked by the usual array of wash and low wines chargers and feints and spirit receivers.

Rosebank also had three separate worm tubs (interestingly, they were still in use a century later), two blending vats, of 1,204 and 2,064 gallons respectively, and five bonded warehouses of various dimensions holding half-a-million gallons in total. The distillery boasted a 150-foot chimney, double-lined to a height of 30 feet, and a vast 30-foot by seven Galloway's double-flued boiler. Annual output at that time was 123,000 gallons.

By joining SMD, Rosebank came under the DCL umbrella and stayed there as a strong supplier of Lowland malt for DCL blends and as a respected single malt in its own right. It was not on the list of DCL distilleries mothballed in 1983, but it was in the quartet of distilleries put on hold in 1993. Although the operational word is mothballed, few believe Rosebank will ever distil again.

It now faces the uphill struggle of trying to be reinstated in an accountant-ruled age where disused distilleries in urban sites are seen as potential goldmines on the property market. Rural distilleries do not face this problem to the same degree. The Camelon maltings were closed in 1968 and largely demolished, although some of the plant is now a Beefeater restaurant, part of the same company which converted Millburn Distillery in Inverness. A similar fate looks increasingly likely to befall Rosebank, for all the high regard it continues to enjoy in malt-drinking circles. Possibly the only glimmer of hope is that a large amount of millennium funding is due to be spent on the Forth and Clyde Canal and Falkirk features strongly in these plans. The town may yet become a place where tourists will visit or even pass through on the canal and there is talk in trade circles that Rosebank could rise on the back of this new development.

On the drinking front, Rosebank can still be bought widely as a single malt of various ages and strengths. It remains one of the great Lowland drinking experiences.

ST MAGDALENE, *Linlithgow, West Lothian*

St Magdalene had quite a fascinating history and was one lowland distillery which survived all the ups and downs of the industry only to be finally closed by SMD around 1983.

It stands, or rather stood, on a historic site. The Knights Templar of St John of Torphichen opened a hospital there in the 12th century, mainly to treat lepers. Later, there was a convent on the site, called St Magdalene's convent or possibly Lazar House, the order being known as the Lazarites. The knoll behind the convent was called Pilgrims Hill.

Linlithgow's first distillery was Bulzion, which opened in the 1750s. At the end of the century Adam Dawson, who already had a distillery near Falkirk, opened Bonnytoun at Linlithgow. Shortly afterwards Sebastian Henderson feued some land at St Magdalene's – adjacent to Bonnytoun – from the Countess of Dalhousie and set up a distillery as well. At one point, Linlithgow had no fewer than five licensed distilleries.

Adam Dawson eventually bought Sebastian Henderson out and, as St Magdalene's was the better distillery, moved into it from Bonnytoun around the year 1800. St Magdalene's thrived and expanded, eventually absorbing Bonnytoun into one big site. The Dawson family ran it for more than a century, becoming a limited company in 1895. It went into liquidation in 1912, was bought by DCL and in 1915 became (with Clydesdale, Glenkinchie, Grange and Rosebank) one of the original five distilleries of Scottish Malt Distillers.

The apartment conversions at St Magdalene show what can be done to preserve a defunct distillery

Under the SMD banner and with four stills, it kept going until 1983, when it was one of a dozen SMD distilleries earmarked for closure. Soon after, it was bought by a developer. One building has already been ingeniously converted into luxury flats, the other is destined to be converted as well. It is a project one can but applaud.

Like many successful distilleries in the Central Belt, it made shrewd use of the transport opportunities of the 19th century. It fronted onto a main road, it had 600ft of frontage along its own railway sidings and it was close to the Union Canal, from which it drew water for cooling and to operate its water wheel. In addition, barges of coal and barley unloaded their cargoes at the distillery wharf. Process water was drawn from a hilltop spring and a 300ft deep artesian well – plus another spring close to the distillery which was used mainly as a standby. Peat came from moors near Falkirk and Slamannan. It had several steam engines, including a beam-type, installed in 1824 and still going strong 90 years later.

In the mid-1880s it was portrayed by Barnard as a big, go-ahead establishment. It had 14 washbacks, all with 6,500 gallon capacity, a 9,000 gallon wash charger and five stills with a total capacity of 14,500 gallons. Annual output was 200,000 to 225,000 gallons. It had 40 staff and four excisemen, the chief being the quaintly-named Mr Allice Robertson.

St Magdalene is one lost distillery whose malt can still be had from specialist bottlers. Cognoscenti describe it as an excellent lowland malt, though virtually all output went for blending.

STRATHMORE,
Cambus, Clackmannanshire

This was the smallest and shortest-lived of the Clackmannanshire grain distilleries, though in its time Strathmore was a thriving operation. It was originally Robert Knox's Forth Brewery, which lay near the giant Cambus Distillery. After the brewery closed, it was bought in 1957 by George Christie's North of Scotland Distilling Company Ltd. Interestingly, North of Scotland was a name used by Aberdeen's Bon-Accord distillery in the 1890s.

George Christie is one of the whisky world's great characters in an industry awash with them. He converted the brewery to distilling in 1957-58, unusually to produce 'silent' or patent-still malt whisky.

However, after two years, production proved uneconomical and the plant was converted to grain distilling using three EPV grain stills. With all three running, they could handle 7,000 gallons of wash an hour, giving an average output of 60,000 gallons of 95 per cent spirit a week.

An interesting anecdote is told about the stills. Apparently the planners had set a maximum roof height when permission to convert from brewing to distilling was granted. When the stills arrived they proved to be several feet too tall. Raising the roof was out of the question, so the stills were sunk into deep pits hurriedly dug and lined in the stillroom floor.

The deaths of three directors in the late 1970s, coupled with the overproduction hiatus of the period, prompted George Christie to sell up around 1980 to DCL. Strathmore was then annexed to Cambus Distillery. Some of Strathmore's capital equipment was re-installed in other distilleries or was transferred to Cambus – which in turn was indefinitely mothballed in 1993. However, parts of Strathmore are thought still to be standing and in use, mainly as warehousing.

George Christie continued his independent path in the industry, mainly pursuing his long-term dream of building and operating a classic small malt distillery. That eventually came to fruition in 1990, after decades of preparation, when he opened Speyside Distillery at Kingussie, not far from the site of the original Speyside Distillery.

Old rail sidings at Strathmore Distillery, Cambus

FIFE

Leaving aside the dozens of distilling minnows which came and went in the 1820s and 1830s, Fife's losses can be counted on the fingers of one hand. However, they are sufficiently interesting to rate a small chapter of their own. They were, give or take a mile or two, the most northerly of the Lowland distilleries. It is also worth noting that one very important early distillery – with a special place in distilling history – stands in Fife.

It was Seggie, at Guardbridge, established in 1810 by William Haig of the Haig dynasty and subsequently run by John and Robert Haig. In 1845 it was among the first Scots distilleries, and one of just two outside the central belt, to have a Coffey patent still installed. It was not an unparalleled success. The still was mothballed around 1852, the distillery closed in 1860. However, it did not pass into oblivion. It became a paper mill in 1872 and – vastly enlarged – is very much a paper mill today. The toll for Fife is:

Auchtermuchty, (*aka* Stratheden, 1829-1926)

Auchtertool, near Kirkcaldy (1845-1927)

Drumcaldie, Windygates (1896-1903)

Grange, Burntisland (1795-1925)

AUCHTERMUCHTY, *Auchtermuchty*

The distillery at Auchtermuchty has several claims to fame. It stood unusually close to the centre of the village, the distillery site was partly hewn into solid rock and and it remained in one family for its century of operation.

The family in question, the Bonthrones, were a true malting, brewing and distilling dynasty. An ancestor started brewing near Falkland Palace in the year 1600 and by the mid-20th century the Bonthrones owned or operated most of the maltings in Fife. For centuries most beer brewed in the county had the Bonthrone name on the bottle or cask. The family were also involved in milling and baking and, centuries ago, in the odd bit of illicit distilling. Their first official distillery was opened in Auchtermuchty in 1829 and, although a modest establishment with low output (around 30,000 gallons a year by the 1880s), it was a landmark in the locality and its whisky reputed as one of the best.

The founder was the patriarch Alexander Bonthrone, born in 1798 who worked as maltster and distiller almost until his death in 1890. He was a determined man. It was a two year task to blast and hack out the rock beside the rushing village stream, with 3000 cart-loads of stone being shifted by horse and cart. The distillery and maltings eventually covered two-and-a-half acres, the process water (from the spicily-named Lovers' Pool) running to the plant via an aqueduct hewn out of solid rock.

Auchtermuchty, later Stratheden Distillery in 1993

When Barnard visited Auchtermuchty (which, incidentally, means 'uphill from the pigsty'), old Alexander Bonthrone was still in charge and then thought to be the oldest distiller in Scotland. He and his wife, Jane, had eight children – two daughters followed by six sons of whom three died in childhood and one, George, died aged 27 in 1885, the year of Barnard's visit. Sadly, the patriarch's two remaining sons (John, the elder, and William) apparently did not get on. After their father's death, John increasingly left the distillery side to William and withdrew into the family home which stood only yards from the distillery. By the mid-1890s they hardly spoke to each other, exchanging cold, angry letters ('Sir: I am in receipt of yours of the 30th ult.' etc) arguing over a few pence in rental or taxation payments. John died in 1901, aged just 46, while William lived until 1919. It appears two of William's sons, Alexander and George, ran the distillery in its declining years after World War I.

Barnard portrayed the distillery as a strange contrast of old and new, the ingeniously modern and delightfully quaint. The copious waters of the stream drove no fewer than three water wheels which powered every pump, stirrer and conveyor system in the place. Yet the two stills were very small – the wash still capacity was 960 gallons, the spirit still just 460. It was in fact an old illicit still, bought battered and dented from a smuggler around 1825 and still in daily use 60 years later. But the patriarch was convinced that only that still produced the right spirit and he stuck loyally to it.

As the distillery and the Bonthrones prospered, a block of offices for staff and excisemen was built, and the family acquired a large house nearby called Cross House (because it stood at The Cross), with direct access from its garden to the distillery.

In all, three generations of Bonthrones ran the distillery. It weathered the Edwardian downturn, struggled though World War I but survived only a few more years before irrevocably closing in 1926. Unusually, however, it was not bought out by either DCL or SMD. At some point in its history, the distillery adopted the name Stratheden (it stood of course in Stratheden) and certainly its letterheads in the 1890s bear that name.

In the ensuing years the family moved and scattered. The last of the immediate line was Miss May Sherratt, a daughter of John's eldest daughter, Mary Ann, who married one Charles Sherratt who lived in Cross House. Miss Sherratt was a major figure in the town until her death in the winter of 1992-93. She was a great character who kept a extensive store of archival material on the distillery and the family.

Most of the buildings remain. The maltings and warehouses are now a mill run by Lothian Barley, the office building is used by Auchtermuchty Community Council and The Cross was bought in early 1993 by the adjacent hotel. A belated moment of glory came in an episode of the new TV series of *Dr Finlay's Casebook* when the distillery frontage was used to represent an iron foundry. The malt barn and kiln were declared listed buildings in 1992.

AUCHTERTOOL, *near Kirkcaldy*

The village of Auchtertool lies four miles west of Kirkcaldy on the old main road from Kirkcaldy to Crossgates and Dunfermline, now demoted to being the B925. The distillery that bears the village name was originally a brewery established in 1650, with spirit production starting around 1845.

The first recorded distiller was James Liddell and Co, who had the licence from around 1850 until he was sequestrated in 1868. The distillery then seems to have lain idle or in other use for 15 years until one Walter Bartholomew took it on as a distillery in 1883-84. He had not long been in charge when he was visited by Alfred Barnard.

Barnard's description of the place is captivating. Its low white and brown buildings, he said, made it look like a small colonial settlement. Once on site, he described the distillery as 'decidedly quaint and striking', as it consisted of several irregular buildings connected with each other to form a hollow square. A contemporary lithograph of Auchtertool confirms it as a rambling array of rough stone and pantile-roof buildings with two squat, square chimneys and two oasthouse top vents, indicating its former use as a brewery.

Walter Bartholomew was undoubtedly a go-ahead man. On a one acre site across the road, he built brand new maltings. In addition, he built or refurbished a total of nine warehouses. Output at the time of Barnard's visit was 86,000 gallons a year, but that was before the new maltings became operational and with just two low-capacity pot stills operating. It is likely output rose markedly in subsequent years.

Auchtertool Distillery, 1974 (John R.Hume)

Barley was locally-sourced and the whisky was conveyed daily by carts to Kirkcaldy station. The distillery had seven horses in its own stables and a large cooperage where Barnard noted more than 1,000 former sherry barrels being readied for filling.

The operation was formally named the Auchtertool Distillery Co in 1893 – probably with Mr Bartholomew as director – and ran under that banner until 1907. In 1896, the company was acquired by Robertson, Sanderson and Co, which in turn was bought in 1923 by DCL. The company closed the distillery side in 1927, but operated the maltings (doubtless modernised at some stage) until September, 1973. The bonded warehouses stayed in use until the mid-1980s and were demolished in 1988. A new housing estate stands on part of the site – whimsically called Brookside by the locals – and housing is being planned for the rest of the site. Auchtertool is another utterly lost Scottish distillery.

DRUMCALDIE, *Windygates, Markinch*

Drumcaldie holds the dubious distinction of being the shortest-lived major distillery ever built on Scottish soil. Like a host of other distilleries, it was built in the late-Victorian boom and could not cope with the harsh new economic climate of the early 20th century. Although it did produce whisky, it seems to have been a white elephant from the word go.

Built by the Glenleven Distillery Co, it opened in 1896 across the River Leven from the Haigs' (later DCL's) vast Cameronbridge Distillery complex. It was a big malt distillery and at the time of building was almost as large as Cameronbridge. However, few records are available on the number and size of stills, washbacks and other production equipment. Barley, coal and other raw materials were brought in on rail sidings which skirted the Cameronbridge site and Drumcaldie boasted one of the highest distillery chimneys in Scotland.

The Glenleven Distillery Co renamed itself Fife Distillery Co Ltd at or just after the time the distillery opened. By 1903 it was hopelessly saddled with liabilities and was wound up. Haig's bought the plant and used the maltings and warehouses to enlarge Cameronbridge. Men from the Highland Light Infantry were billeted in Drumcaldie during World War I and a vast training area, still known to this day as 'The Trenches', was laid out in the distillery grounds.

Virtually all of Drumcaldie is long-demolished and the site today is covered by Cameronbridge's tank farm, boiler house and a dozen or so modern, low-rise warehouses. Although Drumcaldie is truly a lost distillery, the site on which it stood is today part of one of Scotland's most successful grain distilleries. One could say its spirit lives on...

GRANGE, *Burntisland*

Grange has quite a fascinating story to it – Texas soap-opera stuff rather than the genteel decorum of Victorian Scotland. Like several distilleries, Grange started as a brewery in 1767, the proprietors being Messrs Boog and Thomson, who agreed a deal with the local town council in July 1780, to pay £55 a year tax for permission to supply beer and ale to the locality.

Six years later, the brewery was converted to a distillery and for almost all its 130 years of operation, it was linked to the Youngs, who owned the farm on which it stood. They either operated the distillery or leased it to others to operate. They gradually became one of the area's wealthiest families, owning a wide swathe of properties and donating Burntisland's Music Hall to the town in 1869.

The distillery was rebuilt in 1806 and in 1813 was licensed to William Young and Co. The firm was reformed three times in the next 52 years and was leased in March 1855 to Messrs Currie and Gellatley, though how long they held the lease is not known. William Young became a limited company in 1888 and on 7 July 1914, it joined four other distillery companies (Clydesdale, Wishaw; St Magdalene, Linlithgow; Glenkinchie, Pencaitland and Rosebank, Falkirk) to form Scottish Malt Distillers Ltd, which in turn became a subsidiary of the vast DCL empire. All SMD 'founding distilleries' bar Glenkinchie are now sadly shut, though Rosebank's closure is as recent as June 1993.

Grange could well have closed in the mid-19th century but for the determination (the less charitable might call it the obduracy) of the Youngs. To ensure adequate water supplies, Grange tapped two burns, the Binn and the Lonsdale (or Lansdale), which both flowed down from the Binn Hill above the distillery.

Around 1858 one David Logan started operating Grange Quarry uphill from Grange and his expansion plans would have eventually affected both streams. The Youngs obtained an interim interdict to protect their water supplies, which led to an unbelievable 40-year legal tussle between them, Mr Logan and the farmer from whom he leased the land. David Logan had to install a one million gallon reservoir on his land at his expense (£600), plus piping from the Binn Burn's source at Dunearn Loch. It was not until November 1898 that a final water supply agreement was signed between the parties, duly registered in February 1899. The correspondence file on the matter was said to be inches thick and the exasperation felt by Mr Logan and his lawyers surfaced in their letters many times.

By the 1880s Grange was a well equipped place with much modern plant. Insurance valuation for whisky stocks and equipment was a respectable £141,165 in 1888. That was when new spirit was traded at 2/4d a gallon, with two pence a gallon being added each year up to five years of age. In the 1890s Grange employed a travelling salesman, Andrew Keddie, to sell its Old Burntisland Malt Whisky. He was followed by William Reekie, paid the princely salary of £200 a year.

After his visit, Barnard commented that, for all its old-fashioned appearance, Grange was well laid-out and equipped. Output was 260,000 gallons a year, it had extensive sales to India, there were six excisemen on site and its 19 bonded warehouses had a total capacity of 650,000 gallons. It had refrigerators and cooling tanks in the roof and even had a small gasworks to supply lighting and domestic gas to the offices and dwellings on site.

However, all this was to no avail when the bad times came 30 years later. Shortly after helping to found SMD, distilling at Grange was closed down for the duration of World War I. Production reportedly restarted sometime after the war, but ceased totally around 1927. Extensive use was made of the warehouses until 1987 which were almost all demolished in 1990, though at the time of writing one long byre and a three-storey warehouse remain. The site owner's plans envisage demolishing the byre and converting the big warehouse into flats. Grange's most notable feature – the Georgian cast-iron gates and 8ft wall encircling the distillery – are listed, intact and restored. The manager's house, one distillery cottage and a flatted house are restored and occupied.

The great cast-iron reservoir built at the hilltop is still there and water can be heard running from it under the steep, hilly site in a culvert. Grange may never be a distillery again but there is more than enough on site that bears silent witness to its former existence.

EDINBURGH

Whisky has had deep roots in Scotland's capital for more than 200 years. As the 19th century progressed, Edinburgh's port of Leith became awash with blenders, merchants, shippers and bottlers whose warehouses and offices still stand or are in use today. Customs and Excise and other Government departments linked to the industry were located in Edinburgh. The great Distillers Company Ltd and its subsidiaries were headquartered there. Finally, a whole raft of distilleries thrived and waned at one time or another in the capital.

They included the Leith distilleries of Links, Bonnington and Yardheads (also called Lochend), the malt distilleries of Sunbury, Dean, Canonmills, Abbeyhill, Glen Sciennes and Lochrin, plus the two big grain distilleries of Caledonian and North British. In addition, there was a plethora of small distillers who waxed and waned in the decades either side of the year 1800.

Of all these distilleries, sadly, only one is left today – the North British at Gorgie. Apart from being the lone survivor, it had for decades the distinction of being the one grain plant entirely independent of any of the distilling giants. It is a grain distillery the entire output of which historically went for blending. No spirit is made for the gin and vodka bottlers.

Edinburgh presents a special dilemma. The focus of this book is on distilleries that have closed roughly within the past century. However, several Edinburgh distilleries ceased distilling well before then, but virtually all of them were notable distilleries which left their mark on the industry or the city. The full list includes:

Abbeyhill (*aka* Croftanrigh, c1820-52)

Bonnington (*aka* Leith, 1798-1853)

Caledonian, near Haymarket (1855-1988)

Canonmills (1780-c1840)

Dean (1881-1922)

Glen Sciennes (*aka* West Sciennes, Newington and Edinburgh, 1849-1925)

Lochrin, Union Canal Basin, Lothian Road (1780-c1840)

Sunbury (*aka* Edinburgh, 1813-c1855)

Yardheads (*aka* Lochend or Leith, 1825-84)

ABBEYHILL

Exactly when Abbeyhill/Croftanrigh was established is uncertain, but it got into the books of officialdom in 1825 when the distiller, Thomas Miller, was sequestrated. The lease and equipment were offered for sale the following year. Whether the sale was successful is not chronicled and no further distilling was recorded until 1846 when a new operator, Mr J.A. Bernard, installed a Coffey still, licensed on 14 October. He was little more successful than Mr Miller and the distillery folded in 1852.

It later became part of St Ann's Brewery and parts of Croftanrigh are thought to have survived until today.

BONNINGTON, *Bonnington Road, Leith*

Bonnington has a place in history because it was one of the very first sites in Scotland to install and license a Coffey still. The distillery was first started by Messrs Balenie and Kemp close to the Water of Leith in 1798 and was acquired by John Haig (brother of James Haig, who started Sunbury) in 1804.

For the next half century it was operated by a succession of companies with Haig investment or ownership, its last two decades of existence as a major grain distillery. The distilling side closed in or after 1853, but the warehouses continued in use. They were eventually acquired by DCL and they still exist today, considerably enlarged, as United Distillers' Bonnington Bond.

CALEDONIAN, *near Haymarket*

Caledonian was mainly a grain distillery, for some years the largest in the United Kingdom. Even a decade after its closure, it is still a major Edinburgh landmark looming over Haymarket railway station. Yet, as with so many other distilleries in Scotland, neither its size nor its history could save it. It was mothballed in 1988 and the chances of its reopening dwindle with each passing year. Unless there is an unprecedented change of circumstances, it now rates as a lost distillery.

It was built originally in 1855 on an eight-acre site by Graham Menzies, another of the great 19th-century buccaneers of the industry. Menzies had links to Saucel Distillery in Paisley and had built up Sunbury in Edinburgh to be a major plant. But the restrictions of the Sunbury location meant further expansion was impossible – as was a viable rail link to the site. Menzies, never a man to do things by halves, abandoned Sunbury and built Edinburgh Distillery, a name quickly changed to Caledonian.

In location terms, Caledonian had everything going for it. It stood beside the North British main rail line and close to the Caledonian tracks leading to Princes Street Station. It was also close

Caledonian Distillery, Haymarket

to the Union Canal, from which it drew its process water. Originally, Menzies had two other partners or directors, Messrs Bernard and Craig. However, Craig dropped out in 1865 and Bernard followed around 1879. From 1880 onwards it was Menzies & Co alone and the company came under the DCL umbrella in 1884.Caledonian stayed in DCL until 1966, when it was transferred to the DCL subsidiary Scottish Grain Distillers. When Guinness took over DCL in 1986 and set out to rationalise grain spirit output, Caledonian was mothballed within two years.

When Barnard visited in 1886, he could not fail to be impressed by the size of Caledonian. Apart from Port Dundas and the big distilleries of Dublin, there was nothing in the British Isles to match it. Trainloads of maize and other cereals rolled in daily aboard Caledonian's own railway wagons. They carried 12.5 tons each and emptied their cargoes through a trapdoor between the wheels into a huge sluice between the rails. The grain was conveyed by a series of enclosed augers or continuous screws to 14 grain stores holding nearly 4,000 tons. The maize and other unmalted grain was dried in four vast hot-air kilns holding about 75 tons each and floored with perforated iron plates. More augers took the dried grain to the mill, which was fitted with eight pairs of stones and two huge rollers.

The barley lofts held 750 tons of barley which was taken by augers to two steeps holding 40 tons each. The germinating barley was then spread manually over one of seven malting floors, all 172 feet by 76, and malt was dried in two vast kilns which could handle up to 250 tons a week. In the mash house, maize was cooked in three 'pulping machines', then fed with malt into two 26,000-gallon mash tuns which were 29 feet across by seven deep. The wash passed through a 6,000-gallon underback and was pumped via one of six Morton's refrigerators into one of 11 washbacks. Nine of these held 53,000 gallons each, the two others 43,000.

After fermentation, wash was then pumped through two wash chargers holding around 50,000 gallons apiece and two intermediate chargers of the same size. They fed the largest Coffey still in Europe, from which poured 1,000 gallons of up to 95 per cent spirit an hour which drained into six receivers and five spirit vats, the sizes of which were not recorded. In the 1880s Caledonian also had three pot stills (holding 16,000, 9,000 and 5,000 gallons respectively) and a 4,000-gallon Carter's rectifying still with a 200-gallon-an-hour throughput.

After dilution and casking, the output was stored in six warehouses, described as 'enormous buildings covering three acres of ground'. Most of them were on three decks and had hydraulic lifts. Warehouse No 1 held 8,000 casks and No 2 held 10,000. The others, though smaller, were doubtless on the same general scale. Interestingly, Barnard said Caledonian produced grain whisky only – with an annual output of two million gallons – yet it must also have produced malt whisky: there were the three pot stills and its malted barley production was more than would be needed for its grain whisky output alone.

Other details of Caledonian only re-emphasised its size. There were seven steam engines ranging from 10 to 150 hp, eleven boilers, all 30 feet long, and an array of engineering, smiths', joiners' and coppersmiths' shops. There was even a sawmill and, said Barnard, the cooperage matched that of Burton Breweries. All draff was moved from the mash tuns by auger and dropped directly into rail wagons in the distillery sidings: one long train was filled with draff every 12 hours. There were 200 employees and 11 excisemen under a Mr Halley.

Many of the grain distilleries bought by DCL between 1880 and 1903, particularly those in the West of Scotland, were promptly taken out of production, yet Caledonian stayed in use without a major interruption until its closure in 1988. There were gradual changes and replacement of plant and capital equipment, the rail sidings from the Caledonian Railway were uplifted when Princes Street Station and its approaches were demolished, more shipments were made by road and the sourcing of process water was switched elsewhere when the canal became stagnant and unused.

After Caledonian's closure in 1988, occasional stories surfaced in the trade press that it might be re-equipped and reinstated, although that possibility dwindled with each passing year. The distilling equipment was gradually dismantled and the site put on the market around 1995. However, potential buyers were deterred by the entire site being listed, so United Distillers and Historic Scotland negotiated a curtailed tally of listed buildings, which included the main chimney. Some de-listed buildings were then demolished and by early 1997 there was a serious offer for a mixed commercial and residential development on the site. Whatever may be built, it is beyond doubt that Caledonian is a lost distillery.

Interestingly, the purchase of Caledonian by DCL in 1884 had one significant consequence. Several blenders and merchants, led by Andrew Usher and alarmed by what they saw as DCL's increasing stranglehold on grain whisky production, decided to establish their own independent grain distillery at Gorgie, a mile or so west of Caledonian. Perhaps it was coincidence, but they named it North British, after the other big Scottish railway company. Today, North British – taken over in 1994 and still distilling grain whisky only – has the signal privilege of being Edinburgh's last distillery in a city which was once awash with them.

CANONMILLS, *Canonmills*

In 1780, when Scottish lowland distilling was utterly dominated by the Stein and Haig families, Canonmills was built on a loop of the Water of Leith by James Haig while his brother John was building Lochrin Distillery elsewhere in the city. With many others, Haig was sequestrated in 1788 because of the collapse of their English distributor and Canonmills was bought by John Stein of the Stein distilling dynasty in 1790.

In 1794 – during widespread famine brought on by dire harvests – the distillery was nearly pillaged by a mob who had heard that barley and vegetables were being hoarded there. Soldiers were drafted in to protect the building and the riot ringleaders were eventually arrested, tried, convicted and sent to Australia, which in those days was seen as a dire punishment.

Canonmills stayed with the Steins through other vicissitudes until 1825, then returned to the Haigs, who operated it until the 1840s. It was later used as a brewery maltings and for other purposes and was only finally demolished in the 1970s. Today the site is occupied by the famous 'Colonies' housing scheme in a number of cul-de-sacs off Glenogle Road.

DEAN, *off Bell's Brae*

Dean was a very late arrival on the Edinburgh distilling scene. In 1881 James Johnstone, who owned Glenpatrick Distillery near Paisley, converted a flour mill beside the Water of Leith at Dean Village, a hamlet only five minutes' walk from Charlotte Square. It also stood barely 200 yards from the by then redundant Sunbury

Distillery and almost in the shadow of the Dean Bridge that carries the Queensferry Road across the deep gorge of the Leith. In 1887, during an era of take-overs and amalgamations, it was bought by Scotch Whisky Distillers Ltd, who also gained Glenpatrick, Glen Nevis at Campbeltown, Glen-darroch at Ardrishaig and Ben Wyvis at Dingwall at the same time.

SWD itself went into liquidation in the 1890s and Dean stood idle for several years. It was then bought by Robert Barr who created the Dean Distillery Co around 1908. As with other distilleries, Dean's fortunes went into steep decline in the horrendous period following World War I. The company was acquired by SMD in 1922 and the distillery closed soon after. Its history since then is obscure, but some of the distillery buildings remain, either as private residences or as premises for architects and accountants.

It was visited by Barnard and, from his description, Dean seems to have been an apposite lesson in squeezing a quart into a pint pot. Into a steep, awkward acre-and-a-half site, they had managed to shoehorn all the production side (including barley lofts, five big malting floors, five 9,000-gallon washbacks, a 7,000-gallon wash charger, a 4,800-gallon wash still and a 3,000-gallon spirit still), plus seven bonded warehouses with a total capacity of 2,500 casks. However, space in the still-house was at a premium – the worm tub stood on stilts outside the building, jutting several feet over the river. Annual output was 73,000 gallons. All water used, even for cooling, came from the mains supply.

There were some buildings on the other side of the river as was the main chimney stack. This meant smoke from the boilers first went across the river in a huge cast-iron flue pipe about 5ft above water level. . . Dean may not have been Edinburgh's biggest and best distillery, but was almost certainly its most ingenious.

Dean Distillery, c1890 (R.C.A.H.M.S)

Its history since then is obscure, but many of the distillery buildings remain, either as homes or as the offices of a large insurance company.

GLEN SCIENNES, *Newington*

As a rough rule of thumb, Edinburgh malt distilleries were built along the Water of Leith, its grain distilleries (Caledonian and North British) close to main railway lines. Glen Sciennes was the one distillery which, at least at first sight, was the outsider. It was a malt distillery which stood far from the others in the Newington area south of The Meadows and Arthur's Seat.

However, it was not quite as incongruous as it seems. Newington was one of the capital's main brewing areas and in bygone times malt barns stood in The Meadows. One brewery dating back to 1430, located in Sciennes Street and Causewayside, was bought by Alexander Pearson in 1849 and converted to West Sciennes distillery. The conversion depleted his funds and he was sequestrated in 1850. In 1851 Thomas Duncanson acquired it, first naming it Newington and later Glen Sciennes. It was bought off him in 1859 by the great Andrew Usher, who again renamed it – this time Edinburgh Distillery – and operated it under that name until 1919. It was then sold to SMD who closed it down in 1925. Its subsequent history is obscure.

Andrew Usher – regarded as the pioneer of blending – was also behind Edinburgh's one surviving distillery, North British. With a business consortium he set it up in 1885 as an independent grain distillery to try and break the near-monopoly that DCL had built up for themselves in the mid-1880s.

Glen Sciennes faced an initial problem. It stood on a constricted urban site with no malting facilities and virtually no storage space for malt, peat, coal or barrels of new spirit. However, it was only a few hundred yards from the new North British Railway freightyard at St Leonards and it was there that both maltings and bonded warehouses were built. For more than 60 years a squad of horses and carts ferried malt and fuel one way and new spirit and draff the other. It was said the horses knew the route so well they could have trotted it without the carters, but that folk myth was, one suspects, never wholly put to the test.

Glen Sciennes was one of just three Edinburgh distilleries operating at the time of Barnard's travels, Dean and Caledonian being the other two. He praised the establishment for its outstanding cleanliness stating that 'The copper vessels were as bright as the fittings on a man-of-war' and the simple but effective system for loading grist into the mash tun. A high bridge jutted over the huge vessel and men tipped barrow-loads of grist off the end of it. Sophisticated it was not, but it worked. Barnard was also impressed with the plant's electric lighting and its telephone connection with the maltings and head office.

The production side was unusual in that it used a large number (13) of relatively small washbacks (2,700 gallons each), with a wash and spirit still of 3,200 and 2,170 gallons respectively. Process water was said to come from the Pentland Hills, but it may well have been mains water. Annual output of lowland malt was 132,000 gallons.

LOCHRIN, *Union Canal Basin, Lothian Road*

Lochrin (occasionally spelt Lochrind or Lochcrain) was founded in 1780 by John Haig when his brother James was building Canonmills. The two distilleries were to have not dissimilar histories. Lochrin also folded in the great collapse of 1788, but the two brothers joined forces after the Steins bought Canonmills and Lochrin stayed with the Haigs through many ups and downs (they went broke again in 1810) until 1848. For the last decade of its life, until about 1860, it was operated by C & D Gray, who also owned Glasgow's Loch Katrine Adelphi Distillery.

SUNBURY

When Sunbury was founded in 1813 by James Haig, it was probably the biggest distillery in Scotland. Built into a shady loop of the Water of Leith beside Belford Bridge (opposite what is now the Hilton Hotel), Sunbury was by the norms of the times a Titanic among a flotilla of lesser vessels.

Plans dating from around 1840 show it covering several acres, its ample buildings enclosing four big boilers, two vast mash tuns, 15 washbacks and no fewer than six pot stills. There were three malt

Part of the old Sunbury Distillery, now the location of a furniture manufacturer

stores, two spirit stores, four warehouses, draff pit and dreg cistern and two engine houses. In addition there was a line of workmen's cottages, plus stables, cattle byres and piggeries. On the most elevated section of the site stood the owner's ample house, complete with gardens and intricately laid-out pleasure ground.

The Haigs operated Sunbury until the mid-1830s, when Graham Menzies – who owned the big Saucel Distillery at Paisley – acquired a share. A Coffey still was installed in 1848, coming on-stream in January 1849. But as with many distilleries which installed Coffey stills, the venture was not wholly successful. Menzies bought out the Haigs, but he already was planning to move grain whisky production to the vast new Caledonian distillery, being built up at Haymarket. When that was completed in 1855-56, he left Sunbury for the new distillery. The Steins briefly ran Sunbury, but by the late 1850s it was apparently closed.

As with many distilleries, its subsequent history is obscure. The site today, not unlike Canonmills, is attractive private housing, called Sunbury Street, Place and Mews respectively. One high bonded warehouse survives, called Sunbury House and is the premises of Whytock & Reid, a Royal Warrant furnishing company.

YARDHEADS

Relatively little is known about Yardheads, though compared to some Edinburgh distilleries, it had a reasonable lifespan of over 60 years. It was founded in 1825 by Alexander Law, who suffered the frequent financial fate of innumerable distillery founders by going bust within a year. Over the next quarter century it was operated by Robert Strachan (1827-29), Tom Spears (1833), John Philp (1833-48) and John Stuart (1849-52). In that year it was acquired by T&J Bernard, who were involved with Abbeyhill Distillery. Yardheads was to stay with the Bernard family until the distillery's closure in 1884.

THE SOUTH AND BORDERS

Whether the difference lies in the water, the climate or the character of the people is hard to tell, but distilling never achieved the impact on Borders life, commerce and folklore that it had on those of the Highlands or the West Coast. Even in the Victorian heydays of whisky-making, there were barely half a dozen distilleries in the area. Today there is only one operating malt distillery south of Edinburgh, Glenkinchie near Pencaitland. Recent malt distillery losses include Ladyburn, which was part of William Grant's vast grain distillery at Girvan, Ayrshire, and Bladnoch in Wigtownshire. The latter ceased distilling in early 1993 and initial plans were to convert it into a hospitality and trade reception centre. However, these plans do not appear to have come to fruition, possible due to the distillery's relatively remote location. However, the new owner (an Irishman) is looking at reinstating the distillery and so the stills may yet come alive again. The tally of lost distilleries for the South of Scotland and the Borders currently stands at five.

Annandale, near Annan, Dumfriesshire (1830-1921)

Bladnoch, Wigtownshire (1817-1993)

Glen Tarras, near Langholm, Dumfriesshire (1839-1915)

Ladyburn, Girvan, Ayrshire (1966-75)

Langholm, Langholm, Dumfriesshire (1765-1921)

ANNANDALE, *near Annan*

Annandale was a classic small farm-based distillery about a mile north of Annan, just yards over the burgh boundary. Though spirit was last distilled there around 1921, the distillery has – thanks to the foresight of successive owners – been remarkably well preserved and is a delightful place to visit.

It was established in 1830 by George Donald, a former excise officer, and was operated by him for more than 40 years under the banners of George Donald and Co and Annandale Distillery Company. The Donald family gave up distilling in 1882 and the distillery was leased to John S. Gardner in 1883. He was a successful retired businessman, the son of a former mayor of Liverpool, who wanted a challenge to keep him busy for some years.

He gutted the distillery, replaced the old 16ft waterwheel with a turbine and brought in steam power and new production plant. Process water was sourced from the distant Middlebie Burn, which also supplied the town's needs, but cooling and water for power came from the dammed Gullielands Burn that flowed through Distillery Farm, which Mr Gardner also modernised and improved. He used the copious supply of draff to feed numerous livestock, building up a beef herd and a large piggery.

Other improvements to the distillery included a new high brick chimney (which still stands today, although it is curiously isolated),

Annandale Distillery, 1974 (John R.Hume)

pagoda-roofed kiln with wire-cloth floors and extensive malting floors supported by Carron-manufactured cast-iron columns.

Barnard, who visited soon after Gardner took over, noted four brand-new 3,600 gallon washbacks but observed that distilling was done in old-fashioned pot stills with separate external worm tubs. It is possible that bigger, more modern stills were installed later to increase output from the modest 28,000 gallons a year he quoted to Barnard which was casked and housed in two warehouses built on the other side of the stream.

Mr Gardner did not stay long. Around 1886-87, the distillery was taken over by the John Walker and Sons Ltd, who put in a manager and other staff. Walkers operated the distillery until 1919 – the last year the machinery and plant was rated – then closed it down in the industry's steep postwar slump. In 1919, the brewer/manager was John Grant, the engineer Harry Nixon and the excise officer John Millar, who lived in distillery houses. After 1919, it took several years for spirit stocks to be sold off but sometime thereafter Annandale became a farm again. Indeed, within the kiln a modern grain-drier is situated, neatly fulfilling the function of its redundant surroundings. The distillery has been remarkably well preserved to this day, making Annandale a little gem of Scotland's industrial history.

BLADNOCH, *near Wigtown*

It is somehow impossible not to feel a special regret at the demise of Bladnoch. Among the 100 or more distilleries chronicled in this book, few can match it for the richness of its history and its stubborn ability to survive for so long against such odds. Bladnoch is one distillery about which a small novel could be written rather than the brief pen portrait given here.

So much about Bladnoch is noteworthy. For generations it was the most southerly distillery in Scotland and became the only surviving one in the South-West after a spate of smaller concerns briefly emerged in the county (and also neighbouring Dumfries and Galloway) during the 19th century. It has passed through the hands of countless owners this century and was once briefly owned by an Irish distilling group. It has known long periods of downturn and silence, yet always managed to re-emerge with new vigour. Last but not least, it produced a delectable Lowland whisky.

It was established between 1814 and 1817 by one Thomas McClelland or McLelland and it stayed in the McClelland family for about 120 years. It stands on the banks of the River Bladnoch in the village of Bladnoch near Wigtown and is still today rated as a distilling gem.

Over its first century there were changes at the helm. Either Thomas McClelland, or his brother John, or both of them in partnership, ran the distillery until some time after 1837. In 1851 the partnership was J.T. and A. McClelland. Twenty years later it was Thomas and Andrew McLelland who were later to trade as T&A McClelland and Co. When Barnard visited in 1886, Charles McClelland, the son of John, was the proprietor. The McClelland nameplate stayed above the front doorway until the distillery was bought around 1930 by Dunville's Royal Irish Distillery in Belfast. Alas, Dunville's went into voluntary liquidation around 1935 and in 1937 Bladnoch was mothballed.

It stood silent for 19 years, then was restored and re-opened in 1956 by a new company, Bladnoch Distillery Ltd. Eight years later Bladnoch was bought by the chairman of Glasgow blenders McGown and Cameron, Mr Ian Fisher, who added two more stills in 1966. In 1973 the distillery was sold to Inver House Distillers, the US-owned group who operated the vast Garnheath grain and malt distillery complex at Airdrie. Inver House then sold Bladnoch to Arthur Bell & Sons in 1983 as part of its divestment programme. Not long afterwards, Arthur Bell was infamously acquired by Guinness, who then took over DCL in what will go down in folk memory as the most bitter takeover battle in UK industrial history.

The upshot for Bladnoch, however, was that it finished up under the United Distillers banner in the late 1980s and was one of four distilleries earmarked by UD for mothballing in 1993.

Exactly a century before the Guinness-DCL takeover battle, Alfred Barnard had visited Bladnoch and described a small stone-built set-up on a two-acre site with a 50-acre farm attached. Water came from an upstream dam on the River Bladnoch which turned an overshot water-wheel – the distillery's one source of motive power. There were three malt barns, all with upper floors for storage, the ground floor being used for germinating. There were two peat-fired kilns floored with the customary perforated iron plates.

After removal to the malt store, the malt was ground and mixed in a 16-ft diameter mash tun supplied with hot water from two

2,800-gallon coppers. Unusually, the worts were cooled in the 3,000-gallon underback which was sunk in the bed of the watercourse. However, there was also a Miller's refrigerator. The cooled worts were pumped into one of six washbacks, two holding 6,000 gallons each, the other four 3,500 gallons each. After fermentation, the wash was pumped to the still house which boasted a substantial 13,000-gallon wash still but two tiny (400 gallons each) spirit stills. The capacity difference between wash and spirit stills was the greatest Barnard was to see in any distillery. All three stills had their worms cooled in one big river-fed tub.

Bladnoch had four bonded warehouses around one courtyard holding just over 800 casks totalling 80,700 gallons. Annual output was around 51,000 gallons of pure malt. Barnard also noted a handsome peat shed with iron columns and slated roof and a busy cask shed and cooperage. It was a small but successful family enterprise.

After Bladnoch was mothballed in 1993 there were initial plans to make it into a trade reception and hospitality centre mainly for business and trade customers. That did not happen and UD have since sold the distillery to an Irish businessman who has stated that he would like to see the distillery back in operation. Its future, therefore, may not be as bleak as first thought. Bladnoch single malt is quite widely available at many ages and strengths from specialist whisky shops and the rarer sherried examples which occasionally come to light are exceptional by any standards.

GLEN TARRAS, *near Langholm*

Glen Tarras was a substantial distillery lying beside the Tarras, a tributary of the Border Esk, about four miles from Langholm. It was built in the late 1830s by James Kennedy and run by him until 1872. It was then acquired by the Glentarras Distillery Company, in which the Twentyman family had a large stake. The company's fortunes were mixed and it was dissolved in 1881. Percy A. Browne then put money into the company with Joseph Twentyman remaining manager and he was still in charge when Barnard visited in the mid-1880s.

The London firm of Seager, Evans and Co (who were to buy Glenugie at a later date) bought Glen Tarras in 1903 and ceased distilling sometime after 1905. All spirit stock had been removed by

Glen Tarras Distillery, c1890. Only the manager's house on the right still remains.

1914 and it was formally closed down. The warehouses were used throughout World War I to billet munitions workers from Gretna, then lay idle for a decade and were finally demolished in 1930, by Mr Penfold of Brampton.

The distillery stood in a magnificent setting, ringed by woodlands and hills but, arguably, was too far from the main road and rail line to be competitive as the 19th century progressed. It imported its barley from a number of countries including Chile, tapped the Gaulsike Burn for process water, the River Tarras itself for cooling and power and produced a strong-flavoured malt that apparently sold well in London. In the 1880s, it had two water wheels, four pot stills and six large bonded warehouses where 200,000 gallons and more could be stored. Annual output was about 75,000 gallons.

The site today is almost completely overgrown, but the casual observer, knowing what to look for, can soon spot the odd wall and other remains of this once thriving enterprise. The distillery manager's house is occupied by Arthur Armstrong whose grandfather came to Glen Tarras in 1910 as an exciseman from Yorkshire to oversee the disposal of the whisky stocks and he purchased the house in 1930. The house still possesses no electricity and is lit by gas just as it was in Barnard's time. Arthur's collection of distilling notebooks from 1876-98 and other memorabilia is a remarkable collection which sheds light on the day to day running of a typical late-Victorian distillery.

LADYBURN, *Girvan, Ayrshire*

This was a small malt distillery lost inside the vast grain complex built in the early 1960s by William Grant & Son on a 64-acre sea-front site north of Girvan in Ayrshire. The entire complex cost £1.25 million then: building a similar plant from scratch today would probably cost more than £50 million.

Work started in 1962 but Ladyburn first started distilling in 1966. It had four stills, two wash and two low wines, and the usual equipment of mash tun, underbacks, washbacks and so on. Details on the size of the stills and washbacks has proved difficult to obtain. Virtually all output from the plant stayed 'in-house' to be used in blending Grant's Standfast, although some casks did find their way to specialist suppliers.

The distillery was closed in 1975 to allow expansion of the Girvan grain plant. Comparison with malt distilleries such as Kinclaith (once part of Seager Evans's Strathclyde grain distillery in Glasgow), Glenflagler and Killyloch (part of Inver House's Garnheath complex at Airdrie) and Ben Wyvis (which briefly bloomed within Invergordon Distillers' grain plant in Easter Ross) is hard to avoid. It seems that few malt-and-grain distilleries survive long as combined plant, and usually it is the bigger grain operation which prevails.

Ladyburn may occasionally be located as a single malt from specialist bottlers but I personally have yet to see a bottle. This is one lady who keeps herself to herself.

LANGHOLM, *Langholm*

Langholm Distillery had one trait in common with Dean in Edinburgh – it was built on a singularly awkward site. It stood on a rocky promontory on the east bank of the River Esk three quarters of a mile south of Langholm. It was wedged between the main road and the river with the railway line running past a few yards further up the slope.

The distillery was one of the oldest in Scotland and opened in 1765. It drew river water for cooling and power but its process water came from the Whita Well in the Eskdale Hills above. In the bad harvest years around 1795 it closed and was converted to a paper mill. In 1818, John Arnott restored it to distilling but twice ran into financial trouble. In 1832 it was bought by John Connell, with James Kennedy – who was later to build Glen Tarras – and later John Sibson in some sort of partnership. Both withdrew in 1835. The Connells, in particular John's son Arthur (1830-1918), were to operate the distillery for nearly a century.

Arthur Connell was an indomitable figure. He clashed with the Police Commissioners in 1852 over the distillery's Whita Well water rights, as the well also supplied the town of Langholm. It led to a prolonged High Court hearing in Edinburgh and led to a legally-binding agreement whereby the town got two thirds and the distillery one third of the water. That agreement is still valid today, though the distillery is long gone.

Because of the limitations of the site, the Connells decided to forego malting at Langholm and took their malt from J.Bernard & Co's maltings in East Lothian. They also opted for sherrywood casks and for many years were the only known makers of Birch whisky, said by its aficionados to have a remarkable flavour.

Despite the situation, output was 46,000 gallons a year and they managed to build no fewer than 20 warehouses that stored 121,000 gallons of spirit. They sold it mainly to blenders, but offered it also in 10 gallon casks to customers south of the border, carriage paid. The quoted price in the 1880s was 17/6 a gallon for 5-year-old, £1 a gallon for 10-year-old. They also produced a blended whisky Mountain Dew, presumably sourcing grain and other malt whiskies from merchants.

Being a family business it was able to absorb some of the impact of the pre-World War I downturn, but by 1917, with no barley

The caul and weir at Langholm Distillery, c1900

available, the war still dragging on and with Arthur Connell ailing, they closed down. The main distillery was demolished in September 1926 by Penfold's of Brampton who also demolished Glen Tarras, with all materials auctioned by Walter Gibbons of Carlisle. The warehouses were demolished in 1929 and some of the cottages and dwellings bordering the main road were converted into a garage and petrol station. A bungalow was built on the old warehouses site, complete with large lawn. The current occupier's father, John Tolson remembered the site when it was first purchased by his father in 1927. He looked for signs of the distilling plant but could only find an exciseman's dipstick.

However, it is thought the water pipe to the distillery is still intact and other vestiges remain, too. Langholm's distillery, which survived 150 years, is not totally obliterated.

Glasgow

Like Edinburgh, Glasgow was a city of many distilleries with colourful names as Anderston, Bridgeton, Calton, Doghillock, Finnieston, Gorbals, Haghill, Kennyhill, Rockvilla, Town's Mill, Tradeston, Wellfield and Woodfoot. All of these and those listed in detail below are long gone. There are just two survivors: both distil grain only and are among the biggest in the UK. One – Port Dundas – dates back to 1811 and 1813, when two separate distilleries were founded. They were to amalgamate in the 1860s and the combined distillery was to be one of the 'founding five' that formed DCL in 1877. The other is Strathclyde, established in 1927 by Seager, Evans & Co of London which became part of the US-based Schenley's Long John group in the late 1950s. It has changed hands twice since and today produces both grain whisky and rectified spirit.

Glasgow losses this century are six in number and include grain and malt distilleries plus a couple that produced both. Although so many names are gone, countless warehouses still stand in the city and it is still a great centre for blending and bottling. As anyone will tell you, Glaswegians and the dram are inseparable; the city and whisky enjoy a kinship that will endure for centuries yet.

Adelphi (*aka* **Loch Katrine Adelphi, 1825-1907**)

Camlachie (*aka* **Whitevale Loch Katrine, 1834-1920**)

Dundashill, Port Dundas (1770-1903)

Kinclaith (1958-75)

Provanmill (*aka* **Mile End or Milltown, 1815-1929**)

Yoker (1770-1928)

ADELPHI, *Inverkip Street (renamed Muirhead Street), Gorbals*

Adelphi was established by the Gray brothers, Charles and David, in 1825 on what had been a two-acre orchard. It stood just south of the Clyde's Victoria Bridge on the northern edge of the Gorbals. Taking its name from the long riverfront street which lay just north of the plant, Adelphi was to be one of Glasgow's most successful distilleries, gradually expanding until it occupied one entire side of Inverkip Street. Later vast bonded warehouses – the first built in 1852 – occupied the other side. Although all malting was done initially on site, some was later transferred to Port Dundas, probably under contract at Dundashill distillery, and the malt brought to the Gorbals by cart. Where Adelphi first sourced its water from is not known, but in 1859 Glasgow started a vast pipeline project to run water from Loch Katrine to the city. The distillery went on to mains supply in the 1860s and changed its name to Loch Katrine in 1870.

The Gray family operated the distillery throughout its existence, but around 1880 its ownership was acquired by Messrs A.Walker and Co, who already owned two big distilleries in Liverpool and Limerick respectively. Walkers injected new capital and expanded the works to include a large Coffey still to make grain spirit. In 1886, the Coffey still and four pot stills were all in full production, with an annual output of 516,000 gallons. It had ten 16,000 gallon wash-backs, with two more under construction. Three wash chargers held 45,000 gallons in all, the wash stills 6,000 gallons each and the spirit stills 4,500 gallons each. It had six steam engines – the largest a massive brute of 80 horsepower – and six boilers ranging in size up to 28 by nine feet in diameter. The whole was dominated by a huge circular chimney with a flared top.

Unlikely as it seems, Loch Katrine Adelphi was one of the first victims of Edwardian rationalisation after the late-Victorian boom. It was bought by DCL in 1902 and between then and 1907 distilling ceased. Its history since then is vague, but the distillery buildings were not in fact demolished until 1968-70, with the chimney coming down in 1971. The bonded warehouses stayed in use for many years, though they too are now gone and indeed Inverkip Street itself is no more.

CAMLACHIE, *Camlachie Street*

When Camlachie distillery opened in 1834, it stood in a pleasant suburb, distinctly separate from Glasgow. By the time Barnard visited it half-a-century later, it was totally engulfed by the grim and grimy city. It was built beside the Camlachie Burn from which it initially took its water. Ever-increasing urbanisation made the Camlachie water unsuitable and the distillery, like Adelphi, went on to mains supply in the 1860s and, again like Adelphi, opted for the name Loch Katrine around 1870.

The distillery had a distinctly rocky start, suffering three different owners and a name change (to Whitevale) within three years. Then James Guild junior made a reasonable success of it from 1837-1847, when it was bought by Hector Henderson who rebuilt it on a far larger scale in 1849, took in a Mr Lamont as partner but was subsequently sequestrated in 1852. In 1856 it was acquired by Bulloch & Co, which in 1859 became Bulloch Lade & Co – destined to be a major force in the distilling world. They extended the works in 1863, 1902 and 1903, became a limited company in 1896 and operated Camlachie until 1920.

Then Bulloch Lade were caught out by the postwar downturn and government-enforced price rises. They were taken over by a DCL-led consortium and Camlachie was quickly closed down, though the warehouses were used for decades afterwards.

Barnard described Camlachie as a large operation with six acres of buildings split by a central roadway. It had its own vast maltings on site and, uniquely, dried the malt by hot air heated by steam pipes. No coke or peat was used and one must surmise that the resulting whisky might have been the mildest and most subtle-flavoured Lowland malt of its time. Like almost all Glasgow distilleries, Camlachie was big – it had eleven washbacks, the largest of which held 18,000 gallons. It had four big pot stills with a 300,000 gallon annual output. The site's four warehouses had a total capacity of 4,000 barrels. Last but not least, it had a draff-drying plant, possibly the first in Scotland. The dried and bagged draff, which was said to keep indefinitely, fetched the handsome price of £5 10s a ton.

Camlachie was a go-ahead distillery in other respects, too. It had a big, well-kitted cooperage and engineering workshop, extensive fire-fighting equipment and its own on-site fire brigade.

Not a trace of the distillery remains today. Camlachie Street now has a cluster of small factories and only a water diviner would be able to locate the underground course of the Camlachie Burn.

DUNDASHILL, *2 Graighall Road, Port Dundas*

Dundashill and its immediate neighbour, Port Dundas, were for much of the last century the whisky industry's Gog and Magog – two giants which dwarfed every other distillery in the country. Port Dundas has survived and is one of United Distillers' big grain distilleries today. Dundashill is long gone, with new housing on the site, though the sharp-eyed visitor will soon spot the telltale signs of the lost giant.

The distillery was started around 1812, when John Haig feued the ground as a distillery. Over the next 35 years, it went through many changes of ownership namely, Thomas Harvie; Glasgow Distillery Co; R. Harvey and finally Harveys, McFarlane & Co. from 1841 to 1846. In that year the company was dissolved and a new company, John & Robert Harvey & Co, took over. It was to exist until the next century.

Dundashill stood beside the canal wharves at Port Dundas, which carried traffic from the Monklands and Forth & Clyde canals. Barges brought in barley and coal and took away barrels of spirit. A spur from the Caledonian railway was later laid to the distillery and the place grew to an immense size over the years. Barnard described it as having 5,000 tons of barley and 1,000 tons of peat stockpiled at any one time and the grain lofts, steeps and malting floors were all of commensurate size. The two mash tuns held 30,000 gallons in total and the nine washbacks ranged from 16,000 to 24,000 gallons each.

There were two wash-stills holding 6,500 gallons each and no fewer than 10 spirit stills, though these were small, ranging from 600 to 1,200 gallons, all coal-fired. Annual output averaged 350,000 gallons. The bonded warehouses had room for 8,000 casks, holding about three quarters of a million gallons. Dundashill also went on to Loch Katrine mains water in the 1860s, but opted at a later date to re-source much of its water supply from the adjacent canal. To store it, a huge 90yd by 20yd reservoir was built within the distillery perimeter which, when full, was 15ft deep and kept a big pumping engine running virtually around the clock.

Two kinds of malt whisky were produced at Dundashill, Highland Malt (where the malt had been dried by peat fires) and Old Still Malt (dried without peat). Both were sold as single malts and for blending.

To consume the prodigious amount of draff produced, the Harveys – who also operated Yoker – bought several dairy farms and at one time had 1,000 milk cows on their books, though that total was later trimmed to 400.

For decades, the Harveys resisted the idea of putting a Coffey still into Dundashill, though they finally installed one in 1899. Reading between the lines, one can surmise that the distillery had fallen badly behind the times and the Harveys possibly hoped a Coffey still would turn their fortunes round. It failed to do so. Dundashill was to close in 1902. DCL bought it the following year, dismantled all the equipment and merged what could be merged with Port Dundas. Parts of Dundashill were used as stores and a cooperage for much of this century but today the site is new housing.

KINCLAITH, *Moffat Street*

In comparison to the other lost distilleries of Glasgow, Kinclaith was modern, short-lived and is only 'lost' because it was a malt distillery within a larger grain distilling complex that is still going strong today. In the gloomy year of 1927, the London group Seager Evans & Co foresaw the eventual renaissance of the Scotch whisky industry and built a large grain whisky complex, Strathclyde, on the south bank of the Clyde near Glasgow city centre. After Seager Evans were bought over by America's Schenley Industries Inc in 1956, the distillery was transferred to Long John Distilleries (later Long John International), Schenley's Scotch whisky arm.

The following year, Kinclaith was built as a malt distillery within the Strathclyde unit and started distilling in 1958. Most of the malt output went into Schenley's leading brand, Long John. Schenley sold the Strathclyde/Kinclaith complex to the brewers Whitbread & Co in 1975. They promptly rebuilt the plant, gutting out Kinclaith and installing new Coffey stills and neutral spirit stills to supply the vodka and gin markets.

Available information on Kinclaith is slender. It had two stills and was a highly productive unit, producing a slightly smoky but full-bodied Lowland malt. It is still available from specialist bottlers, but is becoming rarer by the day. If you spot a bottle anywhere, it could prove an worthwhile investment.

Strathclyde on the other hand is still going strong. Although the number of grain distilleries in Scotland has halved over the past 20 years, Strathclyde has weathered the storm and its future looks assured. In that respect, part of Kinclaith lives on.

PROVANMILL, *Provanmill*

This is an interesting, originally rural distillery which lay in a hill-side hollow north-west of Glasgow between Blackhill House and Riddrie, close to what was then the village of Millerston. The area is now low-rise post-war council housing that overlooks the new spur motorway to Stirling. Provanmill lay beside the Molendinar Burn, but sourced both process and cooling water from Hogganfield Loch and an abundant on-site spring. It also took Loch Katrine mains water, to be absolutely sure of supplies.

Like many semi-rural distilleries, it had a difficult life, spending years in cold inactivity. Founded around 1815, possibly called Milltown, it was operated by William Kirkland in 1825, then by John Morrison a quarter century later. Robert Simpson & Co gained the licence in 1852 before it came to Moses Risk in 1860. He at some point changed the distillery's name to Provanmill, possibly to link it with the local stately home called Provan Hall. It stayed with the Risk family from then on, becoming a limited company, Moses Risk & Sons Ltd, in 1894. One of the Risk sons, James, acquired Bankier Distillery at Denny and the Risks were eventually involved with many other distilleries.

Barnard portrayed the distillery as small (by Glasgow standards) but efficient, producing 130,000 gallons a year of pure Lowland malt. It had eight washbacks, a 12,000-gallon wash charger, three pot stills, two being coal-fired, one steam-heated. There were eight small warehouses holding 2,000 casks and 20 people worked on site including the two excisemen.

Of all Glasgow distilleries that saw life into this century, Provanmill's subsequent history is the most obscure. It fell on bad times after World War I, the Risk company was wound up in 1922 and the distillery was bought by Provanmill Bonding Co Ltd, a consortium headed by Sir James Calder. It in turn went into liquidation in 1929. The buildings were eventually demolished in 1952-53 and Littlehill Primary School built on the site in the 1960s. The school janitor's house stands on the ground of one bonded warehouse. Today a pond lies beside the school, fed by the Molendinar Burn which cascades down from a nearby hill at the top of which, by poetic coincidence, stands the Provanmill pub.

YOKER, *Yoker*

Yoker stood downriver from Glasgow, near the north bank of the Clyde in the village, later the suburb, that gave it its name. It was founded in 1770 by John Harvey who was to create a distilling dynasty that was to operate Yoker, Dundashill and Bruichladdich on Islay and which only relinquished its distilling connections nearly two centuries later.

Yoker started operations at the zenith of the high-throughput, shallow-still era when distillers were processing four or five batches an hour to get maximum return from the extortionate levy on still capacity.

Unlike many distilleries in the early 19th century, Yoker stayed resolutely with one owner, the Harvey family, though with occasional name changes on the licence as generation succeeded generation. The Harveys and Yoker almost made it to the 20th century without a hiccup, but in 1897-98 there was a messy, and ultimately failed, takeover mounted by the Welsh distiller Alexander Dempster. A new company, Harvey's Yoker Distillery Ltd, was set up but the Harveys were in trouble. They sold Dundashill in 1902 to DCL and saw Yoker go into liquidation in 1906.

The distillery was bought by a business consortium who in 1913 sold it to an Edinburgh group of distillers and blenders headed by Alexander Edward. In turn they were bought out in 1918 by a troika of John Dewar, James Buchanan and DCL. The latter then acquired full control in 1925 and shut Yoker down in 1927. Although there were hopes it would reopen in the 1930s revival, it did not, though DCL continued to use the warehouses and stores for many years. The distillery was badly damaged in the Clydebank blitz of 1941 and today virtually nothing of it remains.

Barnard described it as a mixture of old and new, where low ceilings and quaint ingleneuk rooms contrasted with 16 vast wash-backs with capacities up to 25,000 gallons, two huge Coffey stills and a Stein patent triple-still, one of the few still functioning in the 1880s. In addition, there were four vast boilers and a whole family of steam engines and pumps. Output, predominantly grain with some malt, was 600,000 gallons a year. Water could be sourced from on-site wells, Loch Katrine mains supply and the Yoker Burn, which wended its way through the distillery on its final 200 yards to the Clyde.

There were eight bonded warehouses, plus a large draff house and dreg ponds. Several hundred head of cattle were fed on the draff at Mr Barnett Harvey's adjacent farm which had state-of-the-art milking lines and a dairy attached. Butter was churned by steam power and dispatched daily to Glasgow.

One Yoker idiosyncrasy seen by Barnard was a 'patent ageing apparatus' which, it was claimed, could speed up the maturing of whisky by some form of heat treatment. Evidently it was not a success as it never went into widespread use.

Strathclyde and the West of Scotland

If one were to put two maps of Scotland on the wall, one dated 1890, the other 1990, with a bright red pin marking each working distillery, the contrast would be astonishing. Although there would be fewer pins on the 1990 map, they would be more in number that you might think. Many new distilleries have been built since the post-war upturn.

The real change would be in the shift of pins from the South-West, particularly Campbeltown and around the Clyde valley, to the North-East, particularly Speyside. There is something about the repute of Speyside which has made it a magnet for almost all new distillery investment. In contrast, the South-West, other than a handful of new grain distilleries, has only seen losses. What was once a great necklace of distilleries ringing Glasgow is now reduced to the malt distilleries of Auchentoshan at Dalmuir, Loch Lomond at Alexandria, Glengoyne at Killearn and the vast grain distilleries of Dumbarton and Girvan down the Ayrshire coast. Littlemill Distillery at Bowling is currently mothballed and is unlikely to be revived. The current owners have stated that they intend to turn it into a museum of distilling.

However, both of the grain distilleries had operating malt distilleries on site, named Inverleven and Ladyburn respectively. Kinclaith, another malt distillery, was built in 1957-8 within Glasgow's giant Strathclyde complex but was dismantled two decades later to allow grain output there to be expanded.

Ardgowan, Baker Street, Greenock (1896-1952)

Clydesdale, Wishaw (1825-1919)

Garnheath, (*aka* Moffat) Airdrie (1965-86)

Gartloch, Chryston, near Garnkirk, Lanarkshire (1897-1921)

Glenpatrick (*aka* Gleniffer), near Paisley (1833-94)

Greenock, Tobago Street, Greenock (1795-1915)

Inverleven and Lomond, Dumbarton (1938-91)

Saucel, Paisley (1793-c1917)

Tambowie, near Milngavie (1825-1910)

ARDGOWAN, *39 Baker Street, Greenock*

Greenock is a town we scarcely associate with distilling today, but in its time it boasted a number of distilleries, two of which fall within the parameters of this book. Two small distilleries started in the 1820s – John Dennistoun in Dalrymple Street in 1824, William Alexander in Charles Street in 1825 – both of which quickly went bust. In addition, there were a handful of Greenock-based blenders or merchants who owned distilleries elsewhere and could list themselves as 'distillers' in local trade directories.

Ardgowan was a grain distillery, built in 1896 by a consortium of blenders (including Pattisons of Leith, John Walker, Robertson of Dundee and William Teacher) under the name Ardgowan Distillery Company Ltd.

It was acquired in 1902 by DCL, which bought several Clydeside grain distilleries at that time – including Dundashill and Adelphi – to reduce overcapacity in grain output. The irony was that much of that capacity was built to counterbalance DCL's near-monopoly of grain production around 1890.

In 1903, shortly after DCL acquired it, Ardgowan suffered a bad fire which lasted for five days and cost seven lives. Operations continued, though perhaps only the disposing of spirit stock, until 1907 when the company was liquidated.

At some later date (possibly around 1914) Ardgowan went back into production, making yeast for DCL as well as grain spirit. It was operational in the mid-1920s, closed in 1926, then reopened in 1929 to make industrial alcohol and carbon dioxide products. It was almost totally destroyed in the Blitz of 7 May 1941, when it burned for two days, its blue flames providing a beacon for successive waves of Luftwaffe bombers. The production plant was rebuilt in a month, although the surrounding buildings stayed in ruins for the rest of the war. It finally ceased production in 1952 after a synthetic alcohol plant was opened at Grangemouth.

CLYDESDALE, *Glasgow Road, Wishaw*

Clydesdale was built in 1825 by Robert Montgomery, the eighth Lord Belhaven of Wishaw House, a dynamic and far-sighted man exhilarated by the promise of the Industrial Revolution. The distillery was described on completion as being exceptionally well designed and well built – and so it should have been, it cost between £60,000 and £90,000 to build, a vast sum in those days.

Lord Belhaven bestowed many other things on Wishaw, including a tile works near the distillery and two coal pits, Quarry Pit and Distillery Pit, in the lower part of town. He also built cottages for the families of miners and distillery employees. Sadly, Lord Belhaven proved a greater visionary than he did businessman – very few of his enterprises made money.

From the start, Clydesdale was leased to various distillers, though Lord Belhaven maintained a stake in the business. Over the years the licence was held by Patrick Chalmers; Todd & Paterson and Alexander Jack & Robert Strachan. None can be said to have made a real success of Clydesdale. In 1848, Patrick Chalmers' Wishaw Distillery Co took over and Lord Belhaven withdrew. That company ceased trading in 1855 after Patrick Chalmers' death. The distillery was taken over by J.Munro Mackenzie, who was Chalmers' son-in-law and the first man to make Clydesdale pay. He sought and got mains water supply (52,000 gallons a week) in 1876 and built big

Clydesdale Distillery bonds, 1973 (John R.Hume)

new warehouses in 1891-92. Clydesdale's Lowland Malt whisky also built up a strong reputation under his stewardship.

He ran Clydesdale under Chalmers' name until 1870, then traded under his own name until 1894, when the firm was incorporated as Clydesdale Distillery Co Ltd. With four other distilleries it founded Scottish Malt Distillers in the dark days of 1914. Clydesdale closed as a distillery in 1919 about the time SMD was absorbed by the DCL. Its bonded warehouses were used for many years, troops were garrisoned there during World War II and its use as bonds resumed until the mid-1980s. After DCL's takeover by Guinness, the premises were surplus to requirements and were demolished in 1988 and the site redeveloped.

Barnard saw it as a big, busy distillery with four granaries, eight malting floors and three peat kilns fired by peats from the nearby Greenhead Moss. It had a 15,000-gallon mash tun, four 18,000 gallon washbacks, a wash charger of identical capacity and four pot stills, ranging from 5,000 down to 1,000 gallons. Like most Lowland distilleries, it used triple distillation.

He noted no fewer than 10 warehouses (and this was before the 1891 extensions) which held 3,500 casks. The distillery had its own cooperage and bought large numbers of empty sherry casks for reconditioning and filling. The works had its own direct rail siding from the Caledonian Railway. There were 40 employees in all, including five excisemen. Annual output was 170,000 gallons.

Clydesdale is a particular loss. It was a thriving successful distillery that put Wishaw very much on the whisky map; the Clydesdale label was highly respected in its time. The buildings were said to be handsome and solid, the masonry outstanding. All is gone now and the site is acres of rubble hemmed in by roads and a rail embankment. It has been earmarked for development, probably as a supermarket.

GARNHEATH, *Airdrie*

Garnheath was a most unusual distillery. Its lifespan of 21 years was among the shortest, its location in Airdrie not noted for its distilling pedigree. Most unusually, it was not some ramshackle 19th century satanic mill but a state-of-the-art modern distillery opened in 1965 and unceremoniously closed and demolished in the 1980s.

Publicker Industries of Philadelphia launched the Inver House whisky brand in the USA in 1956. It was very successful and the firm decided to establish its own grain and malt distillery in Scotland in 1964. It bought and converted the disused Moffat Paper Mills at Airdrie into Garnheath (grain) and Glen Flagler and Killyloch (malt) distilleries within one large complex. In addition, there were 32 warehouses, a cooperage plus blending and bottling plants. Simultaneously, the vast Moffat Maltings were built which, it is claimed, became the largest commercial malting plant in Europe.

However, after the great 1960s boom came more adverse and less-settled times. Killyloch production stopped in the early 1970s, Glen Flagler followed suit 10 years later. Moffat Maltings were sold to Associated British Maltsters in 1978 and Inver House bought Bladnoch in Wigtownshire in 1973 only to sell it to Arthur Bell & Sons Ltd in 1983. It also bought and sold the Loch Lomond distillery at Alexandria in the mid-1980s to Glen Catrine Bonded Warehouse Ltd.

Inver House was badly hit by grain-spirit overcapacity and the general downturn of the early 1980s – but more than any other company it took radical steps to tackle its problems. Glenflagler was closed in July 1985, Garnheath in July 1986. In January 1988 there was a management buy-out by the four UK directors for £8.2million and Garnheath distillery was demolished that same year. The maltings have also disappeared as has the bottling plant – though there are now 37 warehouses.

Despite these setbacks, Inver House is thriving at Airdrie, marketing a dozen products including Catto's whisky and has won Queen's Awards for exports. In 1989 it acquired Knockdhu distillery near Keith and Speyburn at Rothes in 1992. But of the vast Garnheath distillery, hardly a vestige remains, though the 37 dark warehouses fill an entire hillside.

GARTLOCH, *Chryston, near Garnkirk*

Information on this grain distillery is scant. It was built in 1897-98 by Northern Distilleries Ltd (who owned Gerston II/ Ben Morven in Caithness), but the firm promptly went bankrupt in 1900. Its assets went to the bondholders, who in 1901-02 sold Gartloch to James Calder and Co Ltd, who already had the big grain distillery at

Bo'ness. Gartloch was run for the next 20 years by Calders as Gartloch Distilleries Ltd. After the death of James Calder senior in 1917, Bo'ness and Gartloch were sold in 1920 to DCL which closed them both. The warehouses at Gartloch were to remain in use for some years but are today long gone.

GLENPATRICK, *Elderslie, Paisley*

In contrast to Gartloch, a great deal is known about Glenpatrick, largely thanks to the efforts of a local historian. Whereas most 19th century distilleries in the Glasgow area were big, industrial and urban, Glenpatrick was small, modest and rural. Unfortunately, it was never very successful and closed a century ago.

The distillery was built by Alexander Speirs, Laird of Elderslie estates, in 1833 beside the Patrickburn which flows down the Gleniffer Braes from Hartfield Moss to the Black Cart river, and was leased to distiller James Hodge at Martinmas 1833 for 19 years at £35 a year.

Production got under way quite smartly, for the half-year Excise return of April 1834 showed 5,809 gallons. However, Hodge could not make ends meet, wound up the business voluntarily in May, 1837, and moved to Campbeltown as a mashman at Lochhead distillery. He was succeeded by James McFarlane, of a well known distilling family related to the Harveys. He operated Glenpatrick until 1845, when the bigger Loanwells Distillery in Paisley became vacant after the death of a namesake relative.

McFarlane and his family moved to Loanwells and Glenpatrick was sub-leased to James Guild and his son, William. Mr Guild senior was an experienced distiller, with years at Glasgow's Wellfield and Calton distilleries under his belt. He retired in 1848 and William took on young William King, then 28, as a partner. King bought Guild out in March, 1851, for £941 and set on expansion, opening a spirit cellar in Glasgow in 1853.

King seems to have been an utter rogue and business woes soon piled up. He went bankrupt in January 1854 owing £3,123, almost half of it to his father-in-law, a grain merchant called Guill. The distillery, after a brief enforced idleness, was then leased to John Morrison, a mature and competent 52 year old, who ran Glenpatrick for 10 years, changing its name in 1858 to Glennifer, which it stayed until it finally closed in 1894.

In 1862, a long-idle textile mill downstream from Glenpatrick was bought by an American entrepreneur, Arthur Francis Stoddard, who turned it over to weaving carpets and eventually sold them in all five continents. Much of that success was due to a salesman, Charles Bine Renshaw, later Sir Charles Renshaw, who eventually directed the company and who acquired many properties around the mill, the distillery and nearby Glenpatrick House among them.

Sometime after 1871, distillery lease passed to James Johnstone, of another well known distilling family, who was to operate Gleniffer and, after 1882, Dean distillery in Edinburgh. In 1887, five distilleries – Gleniffer/Glenpatrick, Dean, Glendarroch at Ardrishaig, Ben Wyvis at Dingwall and Glen Nevis at Campbeltown – were brought into a consortium called Scotch Whisky Distillers Limited.

Gleniffer's final operational years are obscure. The Johnstones continued to live at Glenpatrick House but the distillery was transferred by SWD to Duncan McCallum, formerly of Glen Nevis, who registered as the Glenpatrick Distillery Company. It finally ceased distilling in mid-1894 and has since fallen totally into ruin, though Glenpatrick House and Gleniffer House still stand. The former distillery site is wholly overgrown and enshrouded in trees.

In the mid-1880s, the distillery was portrayed as small, quaint and old-fashioned, with a large millwheel providing the only motive power for such machinery as was there. It had three warehouses, stabling for its carthorses and a cluster of cottages for workers and the exciseman. Output was 70,000 gallons a year. Had it been in the Highlands, it might have survived. Being near the giant distilleries of Glasgow meant its days were numbered.

GREENOCK, *Tobago Street, Greenock*

Greenock's longest-surviving distillery started life as a brewery in the 18th century as Greenock grew from a tiny fishing village to one of Scotland's main ports. In 1795 James Blair & Co (later Blair & Martin) registered as distillers. This name changed to the Greenock Distillery Company in the 1820s, the first licensee being John Dennistoun (1825-29), who had already operated a distillery in Dalrymple Street. After him came partners John Rennie and John Ballantine, who operated the distillery for some 60 years, though not without the odd peak and trough.

Barnard described it as a very old-fashioned place, with triple-distilling in venerable small pot stills and most work still done wholly by hand. In spite of that, output was a not inconsiderable 130,000 gallons a year. Some time after his visit, operations in Tobago Street must have ceased and the plant stood idle for some time.

About 1894, possibly earlier, the distillery was bought by R.Thorne and Sons Ltd, a firm established by Robert Thorne in 1831 and incorporated in 1892. In that year they also acquired the Aberlour-Glenlivet Distillery. In the 1890s, Thornes were in a head-long gallop for growth. In 1896 they expanded and rebuilt the Tobago Street distillery and started two massive developments facing on to the town's Albert Harbour, a huge seven-storey ware-house – said to be among the biggest in Britain at the time – and four-storey office block. Thorne's had gone heavily into blended whisky and their three brands, Kilty, Old Vat 4 and Scottish Arms, were big sellers of the day.

Thorne's survived for about 20 years but were hit by Lloyd George's 1909 budget and the restrictions of World War I. They folded in 1915, though it may have taken until 1923 to shift all whisky stocks. Aberlour-Glenlivet was finally sold to Lancashire-based W.H.Holt in 1924, but records of what happened to the Tobago Street premises, and those on Albert Harbour, are hard to come by.

INVERLEVEN AND LOMOND

Dumbarton

Another distillery that cannot be wholly described as lost, Inverleven was built just before the war as part of the huge grain distilling, warehousing and bottling complex erected beside the Clyde by the Canadian drinks giant, Hiram Walker. By historic coincidence, the distillery stood right on the famous Highland Line, but it has always been regarded as a Lowland malt.

It was not the only malt distillery to share the Dumbarton complex. Another small malt distillery, Lomond, stood adjacent. Its particular claim to fame was its straight-sided stills invented by Fred Whiting, but which do not appear to have been a long-term success. Lomond was phased out many years ago, though it was still in operation in the 1970s.

Inverleven soldiered on until 1991, around the time the Dumbarton complex was acquired by Allied Distillers. It was mothballed in that year and there are no signs whatsoever of it being reinstated. Inverleven and Lomond must rate as lost distilleries.

The output of both plants was used wholly for blending, for the most part in Hiram Walker's own brands. Limited quantities of Inverleven can still be obtained from specialist bottlers and retail outlets. However, a bottle of Lomond is something I have yet to set eyes on.

SAUCEL, *Paisley*

Around 1890, Saucel was one of the biggest and most formidable distilleries in Scotland, turning out a million gallons a year of grain and malt whisky. Yet a quarter century later it had ceased operations and was to be gutted by fire in October 1915.

Saucel (pronounced Sossil and variously spelled Sacel, Sacell or Sawhill) Distillery stood between Sacel Hill and a street called The Sacel which followed a bend of the River Cart. A stream from the hill, the Espedair Burn, crossed the site and the Glasgow-Paisley Canal, built in 1810, passed within 200 yards of the distillery.

Like many establishments started around the 1790s, it was both distillery and brewery, though not necessarily at the same time. It had a chequered early life under Messrs Fleming and Bochop and then under Robert Menzies. In 1825 it was acquired by James Stewart and Co and that company nameplate was to hang over the front entrance for 80 years, although there were to be innumerable changes at the helm in that period.

At some point after 1830 it was acquired by Graham Menzies whose career and acquisitions were to touch many distilleries, Sunbury and Caledonian in Edinburgh included. He installed a Coffey still at Saucel in 1855, though pot still malt production continued. In 1885, at the time DCL amalgamated with Caledonian, Graham Menzies rebuilt Saucel with the grain distilling side hugely expanded, pushing output up to more than a million gallons a year. It was not until DCL's 1903 foray to take over and close down a host of Clydeside grain distilleries that Saucel finally came under Distillers' vast umbrella. Thereafter its decline was perhaps predictable.

Former bonded warehouse at Saucel Distillery, Saucel, Paisley, 1982

Pot still malt production continued until 1914-15 but ceased under the wartime strictures. The buildings were virtually empty when the great fire, started by a fire-raiser who had caused several other blazes in the town, engulfed the production buildings on 16 October 1915. Luckily, the warehouses and their precious contents were relatively unscathed.

At its zenith late last century Saucel covered eight acres and was among the four largest distilleries in Scotland. It had 20 washbacks, the biggest of them holding 45,000 gallons, plus 18 pot stills and one of the most productive patent stills in Scotland. Process water came from the Oldbar Burn via a two-mile pipeline and a 400-ft deep artesian well was bored on site as a standby. Saucel had eight cavernous warehouses and its own bottling and shipping plant, which churned out thousands of bottles of Stewarts' Lion and Crown branded blend. A hundred staff were employed and there were no fewer than 15 excisemen.

After the blaze and World War I, the massive bonded warehouses stayed in use, in this instance for another 70 years. Finally in 1985, with a touch of historic irony, DCL sold them to the Argyll supermarket group and they were razed to make way for a new supermarket complex and car park. Only the most interested observer could today pinpoint where Saucel once stood.

TAMBOWIE, *near Milngavie*

Early in the 19th century, the peat reek of three small rural distilleries scented the atmosphere on the hills and slopes near Milngavie, north-west of Glasgow. By the 1840s only one, Tambowie, remained. It was to last until 1914, when it was destroyed by a severe fire.

It was very much a farm-based distillery, though well downhill from Tambowie farm proper, which still exists today. Barnard found it a well equipped and self-sufficient place, with modern, vertical-type wort coolers, a Steel's mashing machine and other equipment. Compared to most distilleries in the Glasgow area, volumes were small. The pot stills were 1,730 and 1,230 gallons respectively, the annual output 48,000 gallons. Tambowie boasted only two warehouses, one half-submerged, to shelter its output.

Compared to the constant turnover of leaseholders and licensees at many other small distilleries, Tambowie had a singularly smooth initial existence. Alexander Graham distilled from 1825-60, followed by Alexander Buchanan (1867-1884), who was sequestrated. His successors fared little better. There were the short-lived David Chrystal (1887) and Alexander Ferguson (1890-91); the McNabs (1896-1903) and the Tambowie Distillery Co for its remaining decade.

It is said the 1914 conflagration attracted villagers from miles around who rolled up with tin buckets and containers of every description to salvage whisky pouring out of ruptured casks in the warehouse. Some then disappeared into the woods every night for weeks afterwards to enjoy their liquid spoils.

The distillery stood gutted until 1921 when it was demolished. The system used was rudimentary but effective. A big chain was looped round the building and to the tailhook of a lorry which ran downhill and jerked the buildings down in the process.

In mid-demolition the workmen were having an afternoon tea break in the semi-sunken warehouse when a wall collapsed on two of them, killing one and seriously injuring the other. The latter was immediately fetched by ambulance but the dead man lay for hours until a hearse could be found to collect his body.

Today, the sloping distillery site is covered by a copse of deciduous trees. The houses of the manager and exciseman plus a couple of workers' cottages still stand, though much altered. The pond uphill from the distillery is still there, green with lilies and other plants, though the burn flowing from it is fully culverted. The low brick walls of the distillery piggery are visible. And, depending on the crop planted or the angle of the sun, the faint outline of the two demolished warehouses can just be seen in the undulating meadow where they once stood.

West Highlands Islands And Islay

Distillery losses here were not too dramatic over the course of the last century. The real calamity was at Campbeltown, the subject of our final chapter. Throughout the Western Highlands dozens of tiny bothy distilleries, the vast majority of them illicit, came and went in the 18th and 19th centuries.

Island distilleries lay idle for decades on end – the most notable being Jura, which stood cold and ruined from 1915-63, and Ledaig at Tobermory, silent from 1930-72 and inactive for two or three periods since. It has been distilling from May 1990 onwards and is now under the ownership of Burn Stewart Distillers. But, surprisingly, losses of big notable distilleries this century are few and far between. There have been a couple of distillery losses on Islay, attributable to two small distilleries combining with two adjacent ones.

Malt Mill Distillery, Lagavulin, 1964

One of these was Malt Mill, built in 1908 as an addition to Lagavulin but with separate washbacks and stills producing an entirely different whisky. The operation was discontinued in 1960 and Malt Mill was absorbed into the Lagavulin complex in 1962. The other was Ardenistiel, a distillery adjacent to Laphroaig. It had a brief independent history (1837-48) and was eventually acquired and absorbed by Laphroaig. Perhaps the largest loss is Port Ellen Distillery which closed in 1983 and whose fate now appears to be sealed.

Glendarroch (*aka* Glenfyne, Glengilp, Glengilph), Ardrishaig, Argyll (1831-1937)

Glenlochy, Fort William (1898-1983)

Lochindaal, Port Charlotte, Islay (1829-1929)

Nevis, Fort William (1878-1908)

Port Ellen, Islay (1829-1983)

GLENDARROCH, *Ardrishaig, Argyll*

In whisky terms, a wit might describe Argyll as somewhat bottom heavy. For a century it had 20 or more distilleries shoehorned into Campbeltown, but just a handful of other distilleries in the whole vast, water-girt county. Among these were Oban, which still flourishes today, long-lost Lochgilphead (1816-60) and Glendarroch, beside the Crinan Canal at Ardrishaig.

Glendarroch opened its doors in 1831 under the banner of Henry Hoey & Co's Glenfyne Distillery. Over the decades, it was to pass through many hands – Peter McNee (1852 onwards); William Hay & Co (1857-69); William Hay junior (1869); William Smyth (1870-78), who renamed it Glendarroch; Kemp & Co (1879-82); William Gillies (1884-87); Scotch Whisky Distillers Ltd (1887-89), who reinstated the name Glenfyne; William Foulds & Co (1890-1918) and finally Glenfyne Distillery Co Ltd (1919-37).

In its halcyon days, it must have been one of the most attractive and best-sited distilleries in Scotland. Barnard waxed lyrical and eloquent about his visit in late July 1885. It stood uphill from the Crinan Canal below Achnagbreach Hill, which endowed the distillery with two streams – the Ard Burn, which provided process water, and the Darroch Burn, which cascaded down a glen of outstanding beauty and turned the distillery's two water wheels before it passed into a culvert under the Crinan Canal on its last stretch to Loch Fyne.

The distillery was the hub of an entire community. In Glendarroch House and Glengilp House lived owner and manager respectively, with two good houses for the excisemen and eight cottages for exployees completing the picture.

The distillery was extensive, with barley being unloaded from canal boats and hoisted straight into the barley lofts. There was a large steep, big malting floors, a Steel's mashing machine and mash tun, five washbacks and three stills, a 4,700 gallon wash and two spirit stills of 1,000 and 500 gallons respectively. The worms of all three were cooled in one vast worm tub on stilts near the canal, cooled by water from a big reservoir behind the distillery.

Spirit was stored in four warehouses holding 2,000 casks and more whisky was shipped to mature at company warehouses on the Clyde. Annual output was 80,000 gallons a year. Peat was locally dug, with up to 500 tons of it lying in a vast peat shed.

Glendarroch ceased distilling in 1937, though the warehouses were used for many years afterwards. In recent years it has been a fish hatchery – effectively using the large distillery reservoir – and a joinery. Other firms have used all or parts of the buildings. These have now been totally demolished.

Why it should have closed in 1937 at the peak of the late-1930s distilling revival, is a mystery but it is possible it was a distillery that, for all the romance of its setting, never really paid for itself. It was big and isolated with considerable staff and overheads, yet with modest output. For all its mystique, whisky-making is an industry with the harsh disciplines and financial rigours of business. At the end of the day, perhaps the bottom line ruled.

Gone but not forgotten. In 1996 a new blend celebrated Glendarroch Distillery as it was before the turn of the century.

GLENLOCHY, *Fort William*

For one brief decade until 1908, Fort William boasted three distilleries. Today the tally is just one, Ben Nevis, now owned by Nikka Distillers of Japan. Like more than a few Scots towns, Fort William has seen what an up-and-down business distilling can be.

Glenlochy opened for business in 1898 under the mouth-filling name of the Glenlochy-Fort William Distillery Company Limited.

For some years it may also have been a brewery and for much of its life it only knew closures. It shut down during World War I, then from 1919-24 and also from 1926-37. From 1934-37 part of the premises was used by a motor hirer, but in 1937 the distillery was bought by Train McIntyre and transferred in 1938 to its subsidiary, Associated Scottish Distilleries Ltd. Train McIntyre and their assets were bought by DCL in 1953 and Glenlochy was passed to SMD.

Glenlochy and its two stills was among a dozen distilleries closed by SMD in the early 1980s. Its equipment was dismantled quickly and in April 1986, application to demolish was lodged with Lochaber District Council. The application was rejected and for several years the buildings and their 3-acre site fell into neglect and decay, though they were briefly used for a *son-et-lumière* spectacle in 1991.

Glenlochy Distillery, 1974 (John R.Hume)

In 1992 the site was sold to West Coast Inns Ltd, a local hotel group, we understand has developed the site as a hotel and leisure complex. Already a comfortable lodging house has been established. Warehouses and production buildings have been demolished, but the pagoda-roofed maltings and kilns – which are listed – have been preserved and are part of the new complex.

LOCHINDAAL, *Port Charlotte, Islay*

Nearly all Islay's many distilleries stand in the island's eastern portion – that is east of Lochindaal, the great sea loch that comes within a few miles of cutting the island in two. Only two notable distilleries lay on its western shores: Bruichladdich and Lochindaal.

Possibly because of its isolation, the Port Charlotte distillery had a somewhat disjointed life, with a succession of owners and name plates above the main entrance. From its inception in 1829 until 1855, it had no fewer than seven owners or licensees. In 1855, the partnership of William Guild and John B. Sheriff was dissolved and Sheriff continued on his own with a measure of success. In 1895, he formed a limited company in his own name which acquired Lochhead in Campbeltown and rum distilleries in Jamaica. Although it had mixed fortunes, the company kept going until 1920.

In that year Sheriffs were bought out by Benmore Distilleries Ltd, which in turn was swallowed in 1929 by DCL which promptly closed and apparently dismantled Lochindaal. At a later date the warehouses were rented out to Macleay Duff Distillers Ltd, the malt barns occupied by Islay Creamery.

However, there is some evidence that Lochindaal may have been mothballed for some years in the faint hope of reinstating it as a distillery. A newspaper article dated 2 October 1948, on new rateable values of Islay distilleries, listed Lochindaal at £435 gross, £408 net, the lowest on the island. Though much altered, many of the buildings still stand today and the keen-eyed visitor will soon spot tell-tale details revealing Lochindaal's past role. The warehouses have also been used in the past as storage back-up for Caol Ila.

Lochindaal took its water supply from two neighbouring hill lochs, Garroch and Octomore (the latter the site of a famous if long-gone distillery). Peat came from Islay's many mosses. The distillery in the 1880s struck Barnard as a mix of old and new, but its production was substantial (128,000 gallons a year), thanks to eight 10,000-gallon washbacks and three pot stills. There were at least four warehouses across the road with a total capacity of around 5,000 casks. All whisky shipments went by sea, some from Bruichladdich pier, but sometimes casks were floated out to the cargo boats lashed together in strings of ten.

NEVIS, *Fort William*

Nevis was built to augment whisky output from its parent, Ben Nevis. Under the shrewd hand of Donald P. McDonald, Ben Nevis had gone from being a 200 gallon-a-week to a 3,000 gallon-a-week distillery due to soaring demand for its Long John's Dew of Ben Nevis – named after Donald's father, the inimitable 'Long John' McDonald. Both distilleries stood beside the River Nevis and both took their process water from Buchan's Well, a reputed spring near the summit of Britain's highest peak.

The distillery had extensive fire-fighting equipment and no fewer than 20 horses and carts trotted and trundled between the distillery and the pierhead on Loch Linnhe. It also had a big steam engine and modern water turbine powered by the river.

Amazingly, this big distillery was not to last. Either by chance or incredible foresight, Donald P. McDonald took it out of production in 1908 and amalgamated the two distilleries, with Nevis's warehousing staying in use for decades to come. The brand name Long John was sold to Seager Evans Ltd in the 1920s but the distillery

Nevis Distillery, 1974 (John R.Hume)

continued under the name D.P. McDonald and Sons until 1955, when it was acquired by Ben Nevis Distillery (Fort William) Ltd, a company promoted by Joseph Hobbs. The distillery was to close around 1970 following Mr Hobbs' death, and was bought from the Hobbs family in 1981 by Long John International, who spent £2 million doing it up and reopened it in 1985. Alas, it closed again in 1987, then was bought by Nikka of Japan who reopened in 1990 and added an attractive visitor centre in 1992.

One other historic footnote is that Joseph Hobbs' residence near Fort William, Inverlochy Castle, has since become one of Britain's greatest hotels and restaurants. Hobbs, the great bon viveur, would undoubtedly approve.

PORT ELLEN, *Port Ellen, Islay*

In terms of history and their flavour, Islay whiskies are in a class of their own. The island, the most southerly of the Inner Hebrides, was the sanctuary of the famed Lords of the Isles and because of its proximity to Ireland, had long historic links with it. Islay and Kintyre are the bridges across which the secrets of distilling and whisky-making made their way from Ireland to Scotland centuries ago.

Like the whiskies of Campbeltown, Islay malts are – with one possible exception – the most peaty and strong-flavoured in the world. Drinkers either love them or loathe them. Blenders cherish them because even in small quantities they can add such new taste dimensions to a blend. Virtually all Islay malts are or were marketed as single malts, except Port Ellen. Although it distilled a good, robust peaty Islay whisky, virtually its entire output went to the blenders. Only since its closure by DCL in 1983 has Port Ellen started to come on to the market as a single malt from specialist bottlers. Though not as idiosyncratic as its neighbours Ardbeg, Laphroaig or Lagavulin, Port Ellen is very drinkable, as well as being in increasingly short supply.

The distillery has a small niche in history. Shortly after it opened in 1824, it was used to test the newly-invented spirit safe – another invention of Aeneas Coffey – and ascertain that it would not harm the product. As we well know, it did not.

The distillery was built near Port Ellen, then virtually a hamlet, by Alexander Kerr Mackay. He went bankrupt within months and the new distillery passed through the hands of several other family members who had little more success. However, in the early 1830s another family member, John Ramsay, took the reins, won the confidence of the Laird of Islay, was granted a lease on the distillery in 1836 – and never looked back.

Ramsay, formerly a Glasgow wine and sherry importer, had the magic touch and was a true entrepreneur. He pioneered the Scotch export trade to the US, started the first regular passenger-and-cargo steamship sailings between Glasgow and Islay and was still at the distillery helm when Barnard called 50 years later. Ramsay went into politics, chaired the Glasgow Chamber of Commerce and was MP for Stirling in 1868 and for Falkirk from 1874-86.

The growth of Port Ellen and the other southerly distilleries of Islay transformed Port Ellen into the island's main harbour, displacing Bowmore. A pier was built in 1826 and, thanks to John Ramsay, it was improved and extended in 1881. Ramsay became a very powerful man on Islay, owning great stretches of land, building many houses and miles of drystane dyke and greatly improving the island's agriculture.

Alas, he was not at Port Ellen the day Barnard called. The latter portrayed the distillery as unspectacular, with three barley lofts, steeps and malting floors, plus two large kilns fuelled with abundant local peat. The malt was crushed by a pair of large rollers and fell into a 14ft diameter mash tun. The worts were cooled by a Morton's refrigerator and pumped to one of seven washbacks holding 7,000 gallons each. The still house had two pot stills, of 3,500 and 2,100 gallons respectively. After casking, the new spirit was rolled to one of six warehouses holding 3,700 casks in all, or about a quarter of a million gallons. Annual output was 140,000 gallons. All process and mashing water was drawn from the island's Leorin Lochs.

After Ramsay's death in 1892, the distillery passed to his widow Lucy and, after her death in 1906, to their son, Capt Iain Ramsay of Kildalton (1875-1959), a noted ornithologist and expert on the birds of Islay. He inherited the distillery just before the start of the industry's great downturn and, beset by the tax rises and distilling restrictions of World War I, he sold the distillery assets to the Port Ellen Distillery Co Ltd in 1920.

The company, owned by the firms of John Dewar and James Buchanan, was absorbed along with both firms by DCL in 1925 and the distillery joined the vast ranks of mothballed distilleries in

1930. In that year, all DCL's malt distilleries were transferred to their new subsidiary, Scottish Malt Distillers. Under SMD, Port Ellen stayed silent until 1967 – though the maltings and warehouses stayed in use – when it restarted distilling after an 18-month rebuilding programme.

Four new mechanically-stoked coal-fired stills were installed within the original stillhouses, though that system was displaced by steam coils heated by oil in 1970. Three years later, vast new drum maltings were installed with seven drums holding 48 tonnes each. The malt was then dried in three vast kilns fired by both oil and peat over 36 hours, twice the mainland time, to impart the unique strong peaty aroma to the malt – and the spirit – that is the hallmark of Islay whiskies. Port Ellen still is the main supplier of malt to the island's distilleries, with malting barley brought by boat regularly to Port Ellen pier.

After the heady years of postwar expansion came the sales dip of 1978 onwards. Port Ellen was among the dozen DCL distilleries mothballed in mid-1983, several of which are chronicled elsewhere in this book. For more than a decade, it looked as if distilling just might restart there but, although malting and warehousing will doubtless continue there indefinitely, Port Ellen is now beyond doubt a lost distillery.

CAMPBELTOWN

The rise and fall of whisky-making in Campbeltown is a drama that would fill not just one book but several. In all, some 33 distilleries were founded in this one small, supremely isolated town near the Mull of Kintyre. In its glory days, there were two dozen or more distilleries in operation. When Barnard called in 1885 there were still 20. Most of those were still going in 1914 and were to reopen after World War I. However, by 1930 the tally was down to three. Another was to fade in the next decade. Today there are just two left, Glen Scotia and Springbank, and both of them have known long periods of closure. To complicate matters, Springbank produces two malts, its lighter namesake and the more peaty Longrow, named after its lost neighbour, the two being separated only by the width of a lane.

What caused Campbeltown to become the Detroit of Scotch whisky – to the extent it was nicknamed Spiritville or Whiskyopolis? There is no single snap answer, just a series of helpful coincidences. For centuries, the area had strong links with Ireland and its early involvement in distilling. It was both isolated and independent, and it had a good climate thanks to the Gulf Stream. The wide plain from Campbeltown to Machrihanish (the so-called Laggan of Kintyre) was fertile. Coal was mined at Drumlemble four miles from Campbeltown from the 15th century onwards and Campbeltown Loch is one of the finest natural harbours in the world.

Illicit distilling was certainly rife around Campbeltown in the late-18th century. Records from 1795 show 21 known stills in the town, ten outside it. A big maltings, later to become Kinloch Distillery, started at that time and supplied malt to whoever wanted to buy it. The local coppersmith Robert Armour made, assembled, maintained and repaired innumerable small stills and kept meticulous notes in his books of every one, regardless of its legality. The local powers-that-be rarely meted out severe fines to anyone caught by the gaugers.

Therefore an established infrastructure was in place when the 1823 Act took the brakes off distilling. The effect was instant. Between 1823 and 1825, nine distilleries opened. By 1837 the tally had reached 28. A canal had already been built to bring coal to town from Drumlemble by barge. In the 1870s, the canal was replaced by a narrow-guage railway. The huge growth of Glasgow and Clydeside meant Campbeltown had a big and thirsty market close at hand for its whisky. The exponential growth of steam-driven

A Campbeltown distillery interior, c1900 (W.J. Rundle)

shipping meant more and more boats called at Campbeltown, giving the town's whisky-makers a strong advantage over land-locked Highland distilleries. Last but not least, many people had emigrated from Argyll in bad times to North America and elsewhere. They kept in touch and helped introduce Campbeltown whiskies to the US and Canada.

Not that everything in the garden was rosy. For 100 years, the town reeked of peat smoke, brewing and soggy draff. Millions of gallons of pot ale were dumped unthinkingly into Campbeltown Loch, which became an ecological disaster area; a vile-smelling ooze lay thick on the foreshore at low tide, especially at the so-called Mussel Ebb. Many music hall entertainers who cheerfully sang 'Campbeltown Loch, I wish you were whisky' might well have changed their tune had they actually experienced the place.

However, it would be unfair to portray the Campbeltown distillers as just a money-grubbing, irresponsible bunch. They were not. Their collective shrewdness was a major factor in the industry's, and the town's, success. Early on, they established a distillers' association which was both effective and ahead of its time. It lobbied Parliament (its submission to Lloyd George against the massive 1909 duty increase is an object lesson in brevity, clarity and impact) and fought for its members' interests on many fronts without ever becoming a cartel. Around 1900 it pioneered a large draff-drying plant to process, bag, ship and sell draff from all the distilleries. Ironically, one major customer was the German Army, which took 120 tons at a time shipped to Rotterdam. One can safely assume shipments ceased after July 1914.

Campbeltown's distilleries were hit by all the woes that assailed the whisky industry before, during and especially after World War I. In addition, the coal seam at Drumlemble colliery ran out. The mine closed around 1923, ending cheap local fuel supplies. The closure also proved the death knell for the railway, which could not exist on passenger and summer day-trip traffic alone. It ceased running around 1930, the rolling stock and rails being scrapped in 1932-33. By the 1930s just three distilleries were holding on – Rieclachan, which finally closed in 1934, plus Springbank and Glen Scotia.

Before chronicling the distilleries lost in the 20th century, it is worth mentioning those which faded early on. These include Union (1826-c50), Highland (1827-52), Glenramskill (1828-52), McKinnon's Argyll (1827-44), Lochside (1830-52), Caledonian

(1823-51), Drumore (1834-47), Toberanrigh (1834-60), Mossfield (1834-37), West Highland (1830-c60), Thistle /Mountain Dew (1834-37), shortlived Broombrae (1833-34) and an unnamed distillery in Dalintober feued from 1826-27 to Messrs Campbell, McFarlane and Harvey and sold on in 1829.

Albyn, The Roading (1830-1927)

Ardlussa, Glebe Street (1879-1923)

Argyll, Longrow (1844-1923)

Benmore, Saddell Street (1868-1927)

Burnside, Witchburn Road (1825-1924)

Campbeltown, Longrow (1817-1924)

Dalaruan, Broad Street (1824-1922)

Dalintober, Queen Street (1832-1925)

Glengyle, Glengyle Road (1873-1925)

Glen Nevis, Glebe Street (1877-1923)

Glenside, Glenside (1834-1926)

Hazelburn, Longrow (1825-1925)

Kinloch, Longrow/Saddell Street (1823-1926)

Kintyre, Broad Street (1825-1921)

Lochhead, Lochend (1824-1928)

Lochruan, Princes Street (1835-1925)

Longrow, Off Longrow (1824-96)

Meadowburn, Tomaig Road (1824-86)

Rieclachan, off Longrow (1825-1934)

Springside, off Burnside Street (1830-1926)

ALBYN, *The Roading*

A distillery built after the initial 1820s stampede, Albyn was erected in 1830 next to the gasworks by William McKersie, though some records put its starting date as 1837. Throughout its existence it stayed within the McKersie family, the reins moving on to son Alexander and later grandsons John and William. The McKersies were quite successful, taking over Lochruan Distillery about 1867.

Albyn was small – the site was 1.5 acres – with three pot stills, six 5,000 gallon washbacks and five warehouses storing 2,000 casks. Process water came from the mains supply, sourced from Crosshills Loch south of the town on the slopes on Ben Gullion. Barnard portrayed Albyn as a modest, old-fashioned place in 1885, with almost all work done by manual labour. Annual output was around 85,000 gallons.

Like almost all Campbeltown distilleries it was closed during World War I, reopened briefly afterwards but ceased distilling around 1920. The firm, belatedly incorporated in 1920, went into voluntary liquidation in April 1927. The distillery was put up for sale in May 1928 and was sold late that year. Today the site is a modern factory of the Jaeger group.

ARDLUSSA, *Glebe Street*

This was the very last distillery built in Campbeltown, next to Glen Nevis in Glebe Street. The Ardlussa Distillery Co was wholly owned by the Greenock firm of James Ferguson, who also owned Craighouse Distillery on Jura. It was a cracking modern distillery for its day, with six 8,200-gallon washbacks, a big 8,000-gallon wash still and a 3,560-gallon spirit still. Two vast warehouses were said by Barnard to hold up to 18,000 casks (though I suspect he got the figure wrong) and its annual output six years after opening was 118,000 gallons. All the equipment was new and machinery was powered by a 15hp steam engine.

Ardlussa Distillery, 1971 (John R.Hume)

The cash-strapped Fergusons sold Ardlussa to the Robertson & Baxter-led consortium, West Highland Malt Distilleries Ltd, in 1919. This proved just a temporary stay of execution. Production ceased in 1924 and the premises were put up, unsuccessfully, for auction. The company was liquidated in 1927 and the plant stood idle for many years. However, in September 1936 the warehouses of Ardlussa and Glen Nevis were bought by a new company and made into a blending and bottling plant. Today the Ardlussa and Glen Nevis sites are the works yard of a major contractor, and much of Glebe Street is lined with the ruined shells of former warehouses.

ARGYLL, *Longrow*

This was the second distillery in Campbeltown to bear the name Argyll. The first was established in 1828 in Lorne Street by Duncan McKinnon, who died in 1839 and the distillery faded with him. The 'new' Argyll Distillery was built off Longrow close to Hazelburn by Robert Colvill and the brothers Hugh and Robert Greenlees. The last-named was the triumvirate's sole survivor when Barnard visited in 1885, five years before it became a limited company.

It was portrayed as a small, compact, clean and remarkably modern place in 1885, built around a central courtyard. Into its one-acre site everything was shoehorned – barley stores, malt barns, steeps, mash tuns, five washbacks, two small pot stills and no fewer than five warehouses, though their total capacity was only 600 casks. Annual output was just 40,000 gallons. It too used mains water for processing, but had a deep well on site as a standby.

Colvill & Greenlees hit the bad times after the Great War and sold out to Ainslie and Heilbron Ltd, who in turn were acquired by DCL. Distilling stopped in 1923 and DCL sold the premises in August 1929 to the Craig Brothers, who converted it into a garage. It is still a petrol station today.

BENMORE, *Saddell Street*

One of the later distilleries, Benmore was built by the distilling and blending group Bulloch Lade, who operated Camlachie Distillery in Glasgow, with several partners. It was possibly the first in town to put a pagoda roof on its malt kiln. It was built north of Kinloch

Benmore Distillery, 1993. Now a bus depot

Park (which despite its name was reclaimed foreshore, utterly devoid of greenery) in Saddell Street. Early on, Benmore suffered the indignity of seeing its high chimney blown down in a gale: a sturdier successor was quickly built.

Externally it was certainly grander than many other distilleries in town, covering two acres, and had an annual output of 125,000 gallons. Like almost all its neighbours, it was self-contained doing its own malting, kilning and warehousing. Six washbacks held 5,400 gallons each, the wash and spirit stills 2,500 and 1,200 gallons respectively. Four modern warehouses held a total of 3,000 casks. There was also a large cooperage, stables and cart sheds. Process water was from on-site wells, though this was topped up occasionally by mains supply.

In 1920, the distillery was acquired by a new firm, Benmore Distilleries Ltd, who also acquired Lochhead in Campbeltown, Lochindaal in Islay and Dallas Dhu in Moray. Distilling ceased in 1927 and Benmore Distilleries came into the DCL net in 1929. Benmore itself was sold to the Craig Brothers in May 1936 and became a central bus garage for their West Coast Motor Services, which it remains to this day.

BURNSIDE, *Witchburn Road*

Burnside was established in 1825 about half a mile from the town centre on the slopes of Ben Gullion. There were five initial partners, though the original company name was McMurchy, Ralston & Co. By 1840 the distillery company effectively belonged to Colvill & Greenlees, who also owned Argyll, but the McMurchy Ralston company name remained until 1910.

It stood on two acres as an oblong quadrangle. It had four malt barns, two large granaries, six 5,500-gallon washbacks and two pot stills of 3,000 and 1,250 gallons respectively. It had nine zinc-roofed warehouses, 17 employees and an annual output around the 100,000 gallon mark. An attractive complex, whitewashed and semi-rural, its big malt barn was used for a great ball to celebrate one Duke of Argyll's coming-of-age. Burnside whisky was certainly milder than some of the others, as a coke-anthracite mix was used in the kilns with only a small amount of peat.

The distillery hit a bad patch in 1888 after the death of managing partner James Greenlees and was offered for sale at £4,000. One must assume Colvill & Greenlees bought it because the distillery was still under their name in 1905. It faced a struggle to reopen in 1918 and in September 1919 a planning application was made to convert it to a creamery. Approval and transfer took some time and distilling may have continued until 1923. Then it did indeed become a creamery and has remained one, now vastly expanded, until today.

CAMPBELTOWN, *Longrow*

Campbeltown was the first major legitimate distillery to start in the town, as a partnership between John MacTaggart, maltster, and banker John Beith, who was to back a swathe of distilleries in the burgh. It stood beside the short-lived Union Distillery and for a while after 1835 both were owned by Charles Rowatt and leased to Hector Henderson. After 1852, the operating company was given as the Campbeltown Distillery Co.

In 1885 Barnard described it as an archaic warren of a place. Although much new plant and equipment had been installed by the 1880s, it still looked much as it had done during the Napoleonic Wars. It had a 4,000-gallon mash tun, five 3,000-gallon washbacks, two old stills (wash 1,400 gallons, spirit 960 gallons) and four warehouses holding 1,300 casks. Process water came from the mains and virtually everything was done by hand. Output was about 60,000 gallons.

Campbeltown closed around 1924 and its subsequent history is obscure. Today it is a Ford motor dealership.

DALARUAN, *Broad Street*

Few distilleries can trace their foundation to a conversation two men had in bed. But Dalaruan's founding partner, Charles Colvill, once had to share a hotel bed on Islay with a visiting excise officer who told him at length about the whisky industry on the island. Impressed, Charles Colvill gave up being an itinerant cartwright and turned to distilling, with considerable success.

The distillery was established in Broad Street, Dalintober, and took Campbeltown's earliest name, Dalruadhain, simplified to Dalaruan. The original company was David Colville & Co, name after the banker who put up most of the money. Other partners were Daniel Greenlees of Hazelburn and, from 1838, John McMurchy of Burnside.

Charles Colvill's grandson, David Colvill Greenlees, was managing partner (and eventually the town's oldest working distiller) when Barnard called on the three-acre establishment in 1885. Again it was a classic all-inclusive distillery with three barley lofts, four malt barns, four steeps, huge mash tun, seven washbacks and three pot-stills ranging from 2,750 gallons down to 850. There were 16 employees, five bonded warehouses holding 3,000 casks and annual output was 112,000 gallons. There were two wells on site used for reducing spirit strength and as standby for the mains-sourced process water.

Dalaruan had a remarkably undramatic history. It was enlarged and modernised at intervals throughout the 19th century and became a limited company in 1910. As did so many others, it succumbed to the grave new world of the 1920s. It closed around 1922 and its spirit stocks were auctioned off with those of Glengyle in April 1925. The distillery site and some adjacent land is now covered by a mid-1930s housing estate grandly called Parliament Place.

DALINTOBER, *Queen Street*

Dalintober was built in 1832 on a small site in Queen Street but expanded on to a two acre site in 1868 which gave it a 500ft frontage overlooking Kinloch Park. The original firm was Reid and Colville, with three partners, and the two names remained on the shield above the entrance until 1919 when the distillery was one of several acquired by West Highland Distilleries Ltd. Dalintober ceased distilling in 1925.

Dalintober malt, distilled in 1868, bottled in 1908 which fetched £2530 at auction in November 1990 (Courtesy of Christie's, Glasgow)

Dalintober Distillery staff, May 1903. From left, back row, standing: Bob McMurchy, cooper; not known; Dan McTaggart, carter; not known; Edgar Horne, excise officer; not known; not known. Front row, seated: not known; David Colville (b.1844); Donald McQuistan, mashman; Duncan Colville; excise officer?; Mr Pratt, cooper; 'Makum' or Malcolm

In 1885 Barnard portrayed it as an efficient if unspectacular distillery, adding that the view from the front archway was superb. It had three granaries, four malt floors, six 8,000-gallon washbacks, three stills, all direct-fired, and five warehouses holding at that time a modest 1,600 casks. Like many distilleries in the burgh, it had its own standby well but used Crosshills Loch mains water for most processing. As with many distilleries in that area of town, the site is now used for housing.

GLENGYLE, *Glengyle Street*

The third-last distillery built in the burgh's Victorian glory days, Glengyle was established by William Mitchell who traded as William Mitchell & Co throughout. Information on the distillery is slender.

Barnard described it as neat and compact on a two-acre site looking away from the town over gardens and fields. It had just one barley loft, two malt barns, half a dozen 6,600 gallon washbacks, two medium-sized pot stills and three warehouses holding around 2,000 casks. There were 14 employees, one excise officer and annual output was 90,000 gallons.

It too was snapped up in the gloomy days of 1919 by West Highland Malt Distilleries Ltd and closed in 1925. On 8 April that year, the entire 22,500-gallon spirit stock of Glengyle and Dalaruan distilleries was auctioned. The empty Glengyle warehouses were bought in 1929 by the ubiquitous Craig Brothers and made into a garage workshop and petrol station. The distillery itself was rented out to Campbeltown Miniature Rifle Club for some years but was bought in January 1941 by Bloch Brothers, who owned Glen Scotia Distillery. They planned to rebuild and extend Glengyle, but the war intervened and nothing came of it.

It was last in the news in July 1957, when Campbell Henderson applied for outline planning permission to undertake a £250,000 modernisation of Glengyle and reopen it. Those plans also ran into the dust. Today, Glengyle is still the most complete and best-preserved of all the former distilleries in town and is a depot and sales office for an agricultural company.

GLEN NEVIS, *Glebe Street*

Glen Nevis was one of three similarly-named distilleries – the other two being Ben Nevis and Nevis at Fort William. The penultimate distillery built in Campbeltown, it stood on a two-acre site at the bottom of Gallow Hill with a 440ft frontage along Glebe Street. It was in its day a 'modern' edifice though it would have struck us today as austere with rows of small, barred windows and a square chimney with projecting ledges every three or four feet. Founder and proprietor was Duncan MacCallum, who has been mentioned under other distilleries elsewhere.

It had much modern equipment for the era, including a system for pumping the draff from the mash tun to an outside mash hopper and rescuing the sparge water drained from the draff to use with the next mash. It had a large Morton's refrigerator, six 6,000-gallon washbacks, a 3,200-gallon wash still, a 2,200-gallon spirit still and two large warehouses, one a double-decker, that could accommodate 5,000 casks in all. There were 12 staff plus excisemen and annual output was 100,000 gallons.

It was bought by Scotch Whisky Distillers Ltd in 1887 and bought back by Mr MacCallum after SWD went bust in 1889. In 1896 it was bought by Stewart Galbraith & Co, who owned Scotia (later Glen Scotia) and, like so many others, came into the hands of West Highland Malt Distillers in 1919. It closed in 1923 and its subsequent history is largely unrecorded, although the Glen Nevis warehouses were taken over in 1936 with those of Ardlussa to establish a blending and bottling plant. Today, the distillery site (and that of Ardlussa) is a contractor's yard, the warehouses are ruined.

GLENSIDE, *Glenside*

Glenside was built in its namesake road in 1834 by David Anderson and two other partners, plus an ex-Londoner, Joseph Hancock, who joined them in 1836. The original company was not successful and the distillery was acquired between 1844 and 1850 by new partners who established the Glenside Distillery Co. It retained that name, though with various changes of partners, until it became a limited company in 1908. After World War I, a majority shareholding was acquired by Robertson & Co, who closed the distillery in 1926 and put the company into voluntary liquidation on 18 December 1930.

Alone among Campbeltown distilleries, Glenside took its water from nearby Auchalochy Loch, rather than from the town mains fed from Crosshills. In the 1880s it was described as a singularly old-fashioned place, a collection of buildings tagged on to one another. On the two acre site stood three barley lofts, four malt barns, three peat-fired kilns, plus the usual boiler, mash tun and underback. There were four 8,000-gallon washbacks, a 2,500-gallon wash still and 1,400-gallon spirit still. The five small warehouses could hold 1,600 casks. Output was 70,000 gallons a year and the strongly peated malt sold mainly to buyers and blenders in London, Liverpool and Glasgow.

After its closure, it was demolished. The site is now mid-1930s semis built by the local authority.

HAZELBURN, *Millknowe Street*

Hazelburn grew to be the biggest and most successful distillery in the burgh, with a production capacity of 250,000 gallons – though its best recorded output was around the 200,000 mark.

It originally stood in Longrow, with its malt barns in Longrow South, and indeed a distillery or brewery may have previously stood on the Longrow site in the late 18th century. But both sites were less than ideal and around 1840 a large new distillery was built in Millknowe Street, the northward continuation of Longrow. The new location was notably historic – it was reputed to be where James IV's Parliament House once stood.

The original partners were two Greenlees brothers, Matthew and Daniel, and Archie Colvill, the son of Charles Colvill of Dalaruan. Mr Colvill left about 1845 and his place was taken by Samuel Greenlees, though the Colvill name stayed on the nameplate until 1920.

The new Hazelburn was built on a big scale. Three vast barley lofts above three similar malting floors, three ample kilns, nine 6,000-gallon washbacks and three stills in the still house. The 7,000-gallon wash still was claimed to be the town's biggest and the two 1,800-gallon spirit stills were among the first to be fitted with what were later called Lomond-type condensers. In addition, there were three vast external worm tubs.

The nine on-site warehouses could store up to 500,000 gallons and by the 1880s the Greenlees had expanded to Glasgow and shipped a lot of spirit there to mature in their Osborne Street premises. Hazelburn took mains water but also had two deep wells. It had three courtyards and the usual array of cooperage, cask shed, stabling and, unusually for Campbeltown, two on-site dwellings.

Faced with the postwar downturn, the company sold out in 1920 to Mackie & Co, who became White Horse Distillers Ltd in 1924 and were absorbed by the DCL in 1927. Distilling at Hazelburn ceased in 1925, though the big warehouses were used for many years by DCL. Today it is a business park, with most of the warehouses demolished.

KINLOCH, *Longrow/Saddell Street*

Originally a maltings and also one of the earliest distilleries in the burgh, Kinloch stood on a corner site at the top of Longrow. The original firm, Lamb Colvill and Co, had three founding partners, including Robert Lamb. He died suddenly in 1826 and Robert Ralston joined in his place. The company stayed unaltered, except for the odd generation change, until 1919. It thrived and expanded until its Longrow frontage was 240ft, its Kinloch Park facade 400ft.

Its operational side was similar to many others in Campbeltown. Three barley lofts, three steeps, three malting floors, three peat-fired kiln, a big mash-tun, eight washbacks of 7,400 gallons each, a big wash still and two smaller spirit stills – one coal-fired, the other steam-heated. Output was about 100,000 gallons a year. There were four warehouses holding up to 3,000 casks in all, some 14 staff plus an exciseman. Mains water was used for processing and there was a big on-site well as a standby.

After the death of managing partner David Colvill in August 1918, Kinloch was bought the following year by West Highland Malt Distilleries Ltd, which was to collapse in 1923-24. It was then bought from WHMD by David MacCallum, but he only managed to keep it going until 1926, the last filling being on 6 April that year. Unable to sell the distillery, he offered it as a gift to the town council in December 1928 as building land. It was accepted and Park Square was built on the 1.3 acre site. David MacCallum died in Campbeltown just before Christmas 1930, aged 83, and never lived to see the new housing. However, a small street leading past the square was duly named after him. The housing still stands today.

KINTYRE, *Broad Street*

Although Kintyre was registered in 1825-26 it was not built until 1831-32 and was one of the first distilleries to take gas from the burgh's new gasworks. The original owner was banker John Beith and, after his death in 1840, his son John junior set up a new partnership with distiller John Ross and John Colville of the Clydesdale Bank. Its title was Beith, Ross and Co, but that partnership was dissolved in 1876. From then on until its closure in 1920, the company name was John Ross & Co.

It was a small distillery and from 1825 until 1887 was jointly operated with Longrow Distillery, also founded by John Beith with John Ross involved early on as a crucial partner.

Kintyre was a small, unassuming place bearing some resemblance to its Longrow cousin, though the buildings tended to be higher. It had two granaries, three malt barns, steeps and two kilns. A large mash tun fed six washbacks that kept three older pot stills going. Annual output was 67,000 gallons, stored and matured in five warehouses, the largest holding 500 casks. Water was sourced both from the mains and an on-site well.

The same fate that overtook nearly all Campbeltown distilleries overtook Kintyre. It is thought to have closed in 1921 and the site is now municipal housing.

LOCHHEAD, *Lochend Street*

One of the most interesting distilleries in the burgh, Lochhead was established in 1824 by the brothers Archibald and R.Dan McMurchy. They converted an old mill on the Lochhead Burn plus a cluster of adjacent byres and dwellings (reportedly harbouring several illicit stills) into a distillery.

The McMurchys sold out in 1833 to William Taylor and his father, James (the mason at Meadowburn), who operated Lochhead as W.Taylor & Co until 1895 when the distillery was bought by J.B.Sheriff and Co Ltd, who had interests at Lochindaal and Bowmore on Islay and in rum distilling in Jamaica.

In Lochhead, too, Sheriffs had invested in a 'rum' establishment. In 1885 Barnard commented on the distillery's 'air of antiquity', though he commended much of its equipment. The ill-laid-out 2.5-acre site had four barley lofts, three steeps, four malt floors, two peat-fired kilns and the largest mash tun in town. Eight 8,000-gallon washbacks supplied a 3,300-gallon wash still and an 1,800-gallon spirit still. Annual output was a commendable 111,000 gallons which were matured in five warehouses holding 3,000 casks in all.

Around 1900, Sheriffs opted for expansion. Much of the old works was demolished and a vast four storey maltings built that dwarfed the neighbouring houses. The maltings were further expanded in 1905. Several new warehouses were built, the largest in nearby Saddell Street which alone held 4,000 casks. Mashing capacity was raised to 2,000 bushels a week, giving Lochhead a theoretical output of 4,000-plus gallons of proof spirit, or approaching 150,000 gallons in an eight month season. Bigger stills were also installed – a wash of 5,000 gallons, and spirit of 2,500.

With the benefit of hindsight, one can say they did it all at the wrong time. Sheriffs folded in 1920 with some assets, including Lochhead, acquired by Benmore Distilleries Ltd. Lochhead closed in 1928 and Benmore was absorbed by DCL in 1929. Some buildings were used in the ensuing decades but the remnants were eventually razed. Today a Tesco supermarket and car park stand on the former Lochhead site, with two miniature turrets giving a subtle hint of what stood on site before

LOCHRUAN, *Princes Street, Dalintober*

Like Glenside, Lochruan did not take its water from the mains but had its own supply from Lochruan (the so-called Red Loch) two miles from town. The distillery was built in Dalintober between 1833 and 1835 by Robert and Charles Johnston, who operated as Johnston & Co. Around 1867 they sold it to John and William McKersie, who already owned Albyn. They rebuilt Lochruan and operated it under the banner of the Lochruan Distillery Co.

The new distillery stood on two acres with two square chimneys and a high perimeter wall. It had two large barley lofts, four malt barns, two kilns, a vast mash tun, seven washbacks and three stills; the wash still being 3,250 gallons, the two spirit stills about 1,800 gallons each. Five on-site warehouses could store 2,000 or more casks and annual output was 85,000 gallons. There were 12 employees, plus the excisemen.

In the wake of Lloyd George's 1909 duty rises, Lochruan dabbled briefly in 1910 with continuous distillation to cut costs. The McKersies sold out in 1919 to James Buchanan & Co, who undertook some alterations to the works in 1921. Buchanan & Co was absorbed by DCL in 1925 and distilling at Lochruan stopped. The site again is mid-1930s council housing looking across Kinloch Park to the sea.

LONGROW, *Longrow*

Longrow was either the third or fourth legal distillery to open in Campbeltown and was one of the ten or so which failed to see the 20th century. Despite its name, it stood well back from Longrow and was gradually hemmed in by other buildings. It was established by distiller John Ross, with financial backing from those two noted local bankers, John Colville and John Beith – hence the original company name of Colville, Beith & Co.

The company name changed twice; firstly to Beith, Ross & Co in 1852 and then to John Ross & Co in 1876. John Ross was the enduring bedrock of the distillery – and of Kintyre, which he jointly ran with Longrow for more than 50 years.

John Ross eventually died – the oldest distiller in Campbeltown – in 1886 and Longrow was acquired by William and James Greenlees the following year. However, they must have found it a difficult business proposition. It was encircled by other buildings, access was difficult and it was an old-fashioned and under-equipped place. Expansion and modernisation were both out of the question, so it was shut down in 1896, only the second distillery to close in the burgh in almost 40 years.

Barnard, who met the 85 year old John Ross just months before his death and described him as 'a hale and hearty old gentleman, full of wit and racy anecdotes', found the distillery an old and outmoded place, with almost everything done by hand. He described the stillhouse as the quaintest he had set eyes on, with two old smuggler-pattern pot stills. Output was 40,000 gallons a year. There was a steam engine, one concession to modernity, to power the malt mill and the three warehouses were quite substantial, the largest harbouring 600 casks.

What happened to Longrow in the years following its closure is largely unrecorded, but one bonded warehouse still stands today and is used as a bottling plant by Springbank. Other vestiges may well exist, too.

MEADOWBURN, *Tomaig Road*

Meadowburn shares Longrow's sad distinction of failing to make it to the 20th century. Among the first legal distilleries in the burgh, it was built in 1824 outside the town and uphill from Burnside, which was started the following year. Original partners were Alex Kirkwood, a merchant; James Taylor, whose son was to found Lochhead; Mathew Greenlees, of Hazelburn and William Armour, of the whisky still and plant equipment-making family.

The partnership changed in 1840 and in 1854 the distillery was acquired by Robert Colvill, who ran it until 1882 or possibly later. The distillery was certainly closed when Barnard visited Campbeltown in 1885 and records of it are scant in the extreme. Its fate after 1885 is unrecorded. Today the partly-walled sloping site consists of a private house, a garage and a residential caravan site off the Tomaig Road that leads up to Crosshill farm and Crosshills Loch reservoir.

RIECLACHAN, *Longrow*

Rieclachan has two claims to fame. It was the longest-surviving of Campbeltown's lost distilleries and, in its final years, was the only Scots distillery known to have a woman at the helm.

Rieclachan was built in 1825 up a pend at the top of Longrow with four original partners – distiller Archie Mitchell, cooper and maltster James Ferguson, Alex Wylie (of Toberanrigh Distillery) and John Harvey. The chosen company name was Wylie, Mitchell & Co and that name stayed above the front archway until it became a limited company in 1920. Indeed, the Mitchells were the one family that stayed with the distillery throughout its 110 years.

Rieclachan was like a little fortress with high walls and a pair of imposing iron gates at the one entrance. In the mid-1880s it boasted two vast barley lofts, two malt barns, two steeps and a single large wire-meshed kiln, said to be the biggest in town. The small mash tun fed seven 5,000-gallon washbacks which in turn fed a 2,100-gallon wash still and 1,600-gallon spirit still. Annual output was 70,000 gallons which went on to mature in three warehouses with a total capacity of 1,100-plus casks. Manpower was provided by ten employees plus the excisemen.

Despite its small size and lack of transport access, Rieclachan managed to hold out through the 1920s and into the 1930s with fifth-generation Miss Helen Mitchell as chief executive. Even her fortitude could not stem the tide and the last casks of Rieclachan were filled in early 1934. By May 1936, Rieclachan had been made into motor showrooms with lock-up garages at the rear, while the barley lofts and malt barns were being used by merchants MacFarlane & Shearer as a feedstuff store. Today much of the site is occupied by a new Co-op supermarket. With the demise of Rieclachan, Campbeltown's 20-strong panoply of distilleries was cut to two – Springbank and Glen Scotia.

SPRINGSIDE, *off Burnside Street*

Springside was the smallest of the burgh's distilleries, built round a courtyard close to the town centre in 1830 by John Colvill, possibly with original financial backing from the ever-present banker John Beith. Despite its small size (annual output 30,000 gallons), it managed to survive the booms and busts of the industry but finally succumbed in 1926. It remained with the Colvill family throughout and the company name John Colvill & Co stayed above the front archway for 96 years.

Barnard described it as a scattered array of buildings around a tiny yard. There were three small granaries, maltings beneath, two peat-fired kilns, a small mash tun and six washbacks, two pot stills (1,200 and 400 gallons) and four bonded warehouses holding 600 casks. Crosshills mains water was used throughout.

After the distillery closed and its warehouses were cleared in the late 1920s, the premises stood vacant for more than 10 years. But in January 1941, Campbeltown Co-operative Society applied for permission to convert the distillery buildings and warehouses to garages, stables and stores. Today part of the site is a Hydro-Electric depot, though a solitary wall of one of the bonded warehouses still stands as a reminder of what once was.